BRAD PITT

Text by MATT ZOLLER SEITZ

HOUSE OF COLLECTIBLES NEW YORK

Editor Jay D. Johnson
Art Director Eric Evans
Production Director Barbara Barry
Production Assistant Rob Barry, Lori Lindsey
Photo Research Heather Alberts

This is a registered trademark of Random House, Inc.
Published by House of Collectibles
201 East 50th Street New York, NY 10022

Distributed by Ballantine Books, a division of Random House, Inc., New York
and simultaneously in Canada by Random House of Canada Limited, Toronto.

http://www.randomhouse.com

Manufactured in the United States of America
Library of Congress Catalog Card Number: 96-77937
ISBN: 0-676-60074-3

Cover design by Kristine Mills
Cover photo by Karen Hardy/Sygma

First Edition: November 1996
10 9 8 7 6 5 4 3 2 1

This book is an independent work, and is not authorized, endorsed or sponsored by Brad Pitt.

CONTENTS

FOREWORD

Hollywood has two forms of currency: beauty and talent. Neither is in short supply. The beautiful are exploited for the one or two films it takes to expose their inadequacies, then they're filed away and forgotten as quickly as canceled checks. The talented fare little better, stepping onto a treadmill of auditions, supporting roles and near-anonymity.

Rarely does an actor enter the scene with both assets in his pocket. And even when it does occur, any combination of bad luck, poor decisions or overblown ego can conspire to fritter away a once-promising career. So far, Brad Pitt has proven himself just lucky, smart and humble enough to parlay his obvious beauty and talent into what appears to be the downpayment on a lengthy, legendary career. Matt Zoller Seitz's insightful essay and reviews will leave you with a healthy respect for what Pitt has achieved in making the transition from pretty-boy flavor-of-the-month to Oscar-worthy superstar.

Before I turn over the spotlight, I want to thank everyone who inspired me, worked with me or put up with me during this project: Paddins Dowling, Jim Beckett, Tim Kochuba, Randy Ladenheim-Gil, Rudy Klancnik, Eric Evans, Barbara Barry, Lori Lindsey, Rob Barry, Heather Alberts, Matt Zoller Seitz, and, most of all, my wife, Rita, and children, Laurel and Joel.

Jay D. Johnson
Sporting Chance Media

BOOK I

THE STAR

Barely a handful of stars

in Hollywood history have

won both adoration from

the public and accolades

from the critics like

BRAD

PITT

Casting fuels the feature film industry, and casting is ruled by considerations that often have little to do with acting ability. Major studio features rarely get made in Hollywood, no matter what caliber of film-making genius is attached to them, unless a star with the right attitude, the right look and the requisite amount of box office clout expresses interest in a leading role. Stars who fulfill these criteria are often people who specialize in playing a very particular kind of part – men and women who found a profitable screen image early in their careers, marked its boundaries, and rarely feel confident enough to stray beyond it.

This helps explain why an artificial distinction exists between "lead actors" and "character actors." The first group contains actors who are deemed beautiful by society's current standards; the second, far larger group encompasses every-body else. This also explains why actors who, on first glance, seem to have the best of both worlds – conventional good looks and genuine talent – often complain to reporters that they loathe being thought of as romantic or sexy. Their looks and charisma create a buzz that lets them star in big budget films and pull down seven-figure paychecks, but after a string of hits that trade on these qualities, they also begin to feel trapped by their own glamorous images; they find themselves being offered the same roles over and over again, and pressured by fans and the media to remain mere objects of adoration. When they step outside their established images and box office cash registers fail to ring, even the bravest stars will often retreat into the safe harbor of predictability.

Which explains why the list of stars who are charming, physically attractive, financially reliable, dramatically gifted and creatively restless is a short one. Actors who have only one or two of these qualities usually must settle for either fan support or critical admiration. Only a handful of leading men have managed to have the best of both worlds. Among them: James Stewart, Paul Newman, William Holden, Montgomery Clift, Burt Lancaster, Kirk Douglas, Al Pacino, Tom Cruise and Denzel Washington.

And now, Brad Pitt.

Since his breakthrough role as the grinning drifter J.D. in Ridley Scott's feminist road movie "Thelma and Louise," he has maintained an image as one of the world's biggest stars and most beloved (and imitated) sex symbols. Yet he has also managed to leverage his looks to further his ambitions as a serious actor, alternating crowd-pleasing parts in accessible, mainstream movies with odd, edgy, sometimes perverse performances of a type rarely seen outside the confines of the arthouse.

Unlike Tom Cruise, the only superstar in Pitt's age range to whom he is often compared, Pitt does not have a consistent screen persona. He seems a character actor trapped inside the body of a male model, and every move he's made so far reflects that conflict. Like the most beloved male icons of so-called "Method" acting – Al Pacino, Robert DeNiro, Montgomery Clift, and the

Brad Pitt: Class of 1982, Kickapoo High School, Springfield, Missouri. Extracurricular activities: debate, student government, choir, musical theater, baseball, tennis.

young Marlon Brando – Pitt changes appearance and demeanor from role to role, yet he also exudes an old-style movie star's effortless charisma. In interviews, he projects an earthy, slightly bewildered humility that fools no one. Pitt is a smart man; he knows that the public's eagerness to pay good money just to look at him allows him a unique level of creative freedom, so he alternates matinee idol roles in mainstream films such as "A River Runs Through It" and "Legends of the Fall" with edgy work in glorified art films like "Kalifornia," "Twelve Monkeys," and

With no formal training as an actor before he arrived in Hollywood, Pitt found most of his early television work on the strength of his looks.

"Seven." Yet he also seems terrified by the thought that his beauty eclipses his integrity and ambition – that one day his reach will exceed his grasp and he'll have no choice but to appear in an unending string of mindless stud roles to regain his privileged status.

It is not easy in America to have both adoration and respect. Pitt wants both.

A female student asked him along to read opposite her for moral support. The agent signed Pitt instead.

William Bradley Pitt is the eldest of three children, born December 18, 1963, in Shawnee, Oklahoma. His mother, Jane, was a school counselor and his father, Bill, worked as an executive at a trucking firm. The family was Southern Baptist and attended church regularly. He was fiercely protective of his younger siblings, and later spoke of beating up people who tried to mistreat them. And he always loved movies. "It started with the drive-ins, you know," he would tell CNN in 1995. "Sitting on the hood of the car with your family, eating the cold popcorn that your mom made before because it was too expensive there."

His family moved to Springfield, Missouri, while Pitt was still a boy, and his adolescent years at Kickapoo High were not the stuff of legend –

Pitt landed his first real role in the prime-time TV soap "Dallas" in 1988, playing the bad-boy beau of actress Shalane McCall. He now dismisses the part as "feathered hair and spandex pants."

solid but unspectacular grades and forays into debating, student government, choir and musical theater. He engaged in the usual manly pursuits: baseball, tennis, camping in the Ozarks, and of course, shooting. His father instructed him on the fine art of handling a gun, moving from BB guns to shotguns. "It's a big deal in Missouri, the way I grew up, to have a gun," he would later tell *Rolling Stone*. "And damn right. If someone comes into my house in the middle of the night, I'm going to shoot."

After graduation, Pitt enrolled at the University of Missouri, studied journalism and advertising, joined the Sigma Chi fraternity, and was earmarked as a campus hunk. Even then, he knew how to sell his looks, posing shirtless for a campus calendar. He planned a career as an art director, which likely was within his reach since the Missouri journalism program is one of the finest in the nation. But to the surprise of friends and family, during his senior year in 1987 he quit school just two credits shy of graduation, hopped into his Nissan (which he'd nicknamed "Runaround Sue") and headed west. He arrived in Los Angeles with $325 in his pocket.

Like most aspiring actors, he moved through one menial job after another while awaiting his mythic Big Break. He worked as an extra, mostly in B-movies. He handed out free cigarette samples. He drove strippers back and forth from parties in a limousine, and in a surreally chivalrous note, stood dutifully nearby to make sure drunken clients didn't try to steal the women's clothes as they did their duty. At one point, Pitt donned a chicken suit and stood outside El Pollo Loco restaurant at the corner of LaBrea Boulevard and Sunset. (It's somehow fitting that "El Pollo Loco" translates to "The Crazy Chicken.") Passing drivers honked and waved, shouting encouragement or, more often, obscenities. Pitt consoled himself that the motorists weren't reacting to him. "They were reacting to the damn chicken."

One of the strippers he drove around town hooked him up with a respected acting coach named Roy London, whose former students include Michelle Pfeiffer and Sharon Stone. In London's class, he met a female student who was going to audition for an agent; she asked him to tag along and read opposite her for moral support. The agent

Pitt appeared as a guest star on several TV shows (seen here playing a rock star hero of Jeremy Miller in an episode of "Growing Pains") before his breakthrough into the movies.

signed Pitt instead. After a string of unsuccessful sitcom auditions, Pitt graduated to minor roles on soaps; the most visible of these was "Dallas," where he played a bad boy part he now dismisses as "Spandex pants, feathered hair." He also appeared on "thirtysomething," won a blink-and-you'll-miss him part in the execrable Charlie Sheen car theft picture "No Man's Land," made a low-budget film in Yugoslavia, and starred in his own short-lived network TV series, "Glory Days." (Pitt despised the latter, mainly because, as he explained to the *Toronto Star*, there is not always a consistent vision behind television series. "You sign onto a project and you have no control," he said. "A different director comes in every week and tells you who your character is.")

The pace of his career picked up with larger parts in the low-budget youth drama "Across the Tracks" (he portrayed a rock of sanity opposite a wild sibling played by, of all people, Ricky Schroeder) and the schlock horror film "Cutting Class," where he met actress Jill Schoelen, whom he would date steadily for several months. He appeared shirtless in a Levi's jeans commercial

that aired only in Europe. He also starred in an episode of HBO's horror series "Tales from the Crypt" titled "King of the Road," playing a mysterious drag racer who kidnaps the daughter of a retired champ-turned-cop to force him back onto the blacktop for a deadly showdown.

A lead role in a top-rated 1990 NBC telefilm, "Too Young to Die," proved to be the most significant of his early appearances – not because of the movie itself, but because his co-star was a fresh-faced but eccentric 16-year-old actress named Juliette Lewis. He played a Svengali-like thug who corrupts Lewis' character into drug addiction, prostitution and murder. They fell in love on the set and would stay together for four sometimes tempestuous years.

"It's been a steady climb," Pitt told an interviewer. "You move out west and don't have a

Continued on page 18   **15**

juliette
Lewis

b. Los Angeles, California, 1973. **"Kalifornia"** (1993). **"Too Young to Die"** (1990). A veteran of nearly 20 feature films, the pinnacle of Juliette Lewis' career so far came in her role as the seductive woman-child in "Cape Fear." Her performance lifted her out of the lame comedies and teen-in-trouble TV movies that had marked the boundaries of her filmography to that point.

Continued from page 15

place to live and go about it a step at a time."

A giant step came in 1990, when Pitt won what would later turn out to be the most important break of his career. In Los Angeles, British-born

Pitt's first real starring role came in the 1990 TV movie "Too Young to Die." The film also introduced him to 16-year-old Juliette Lewis. They would remain together for four years.

filmmaker Ridley Scott, the acclaimed visual stylist behind "Alien" and "Blade Runner," was casting his latest movie, "Thelma and Louise." Penned by a young scriptwriter named Callie Khouri, it was a hybrid of two genres, the crime-spree road movie and the buddy picture. But there was a crucial twist: The two main characters were women, and they were driven to live as outlaws by the cruel machinations of a male-dominated society.

Their odyssey starts as a lighthearted vacation. Louise (Susan Sarandon), a tough, free-spirited single woman, convinces her best pal, the perky but submissive Thelma (Geena Davis), to come with her on an impromptu vacation. While drinking at a roadhouse their first night away from home, Thelma flirts and dances with a handsome urban cowpoke, who gets her drunk, lures her outside, and tries to rape her in the parking lot. Louise, a rape survivor herself (though the script is purposefully vague on this point), intervenes with a pistol and makes the man back off, but when he makes a smart-assed remark, she suffers a post-traumatic flash of rage and kills him anyway. They decide to make a run for Mexico, but have to bypass Texas because Louise was sexually assaulted there and

Pitt had only 14 minutes of screen time in "Thelma and Louise," but they turned millions of heads.

swore she'd never return. The pair is low on money, so Louise contacts her loyal boyfriend Jimmy (Michael Madsen) and asks him to withdraw her savings and bring the cash to them in Oklahoma City. He obliges, and the women set out again for the border.

Enter Brad Pitt as the handsome drifter J.D., a small but pivotal role that set the film's alternately gutsy and tragic second half in motion. Thelma runs into him near a roadside phone booth – a scruffy blond loner with a white cowboy hat, a killer smile and painted-on jeans. He asks for a ride and Louise turns him down. But a couple of scenes later, they pass him again while driving on the highway, and Thelma starts whimpering like a lovesick puppy, so Louise pulls over. The director's posing of Pitt makes his subsequent complaints about being stereotyped as the next James Dean seem either disingenuous or terribly unobservant. Shot in profile, he's slouched back with the brim of his ten gallon hat hanging low over his face; a big abandoned storage facility looms behind him. It's exactly like the most famous shot from George Stevens' 1955 Texas oil epic "Giant," which starred Dean as the smoldering redneck antihero Jett Rink. (As if the screenwriter's decision to name the character "J.D." wasn't tip-off enough.)

In the car, he listens sympathetically as Thelma complains about her oaf of a husband, nodding and smiling and calling her "Miss Thelma." Then the women let him off outside the motel where they'll be staying for the night. "I love to watch him go," Thelma murmurs, gazing longingly at his backside as he walks off into the rain. He doesn't stay away for long, though. Later that night, he shows up at Thelma's door, gazing at her wistfully as rain drums on the brim of his hat, like Burt Lancaster visiting Deborah Kerr's bungalow in "From Here to Eternity."

Louise is away communing with her boyfriend, so Thelma invites the hitcher inside. They flirt and play slap-hands. J.D. complains that Thelma has an unfair advantage because of her wedding ring, and he slowly slides it off her finger, then nonchalantly drops it in a nearby drinking glass. "I think that's better," he says, smiling conspiratorially. "What d'you think?"

He reveals himself to be a formerly incarcerated small time robber – a gentleman bandit with a folksy spiel that he recites to Thelma in a singsongy drawl. "First you pick your place, right?" he purrs. "Then I just sit back and watch for a little while, waiting for the right moment to make my move. That's something you gotta know up here." He points to his temple. "That shit cannot be taught." He hops off the bed and plays the rest of the spiel like an actor at an audition. "Then I kinda waltz right in and say, 'Ladies! Gentlemen! Let's see who wins the prize for keeping their cool. Simon says everybody down

Pitt and Lewis teamed again two years later in "Kalifornia," playing a pair of low-rent serial killers. Some theaters refused to book the film because of its violence.

on the floor. Nobody loses their head, nobody loses their head. Uh, you, sir!" he says, pointing at an imaginary bystander, "Yeah, you do the honors! Take that cash and put it in that bag right there and you got an amazing story to tell your friends. If not, you got a tag on your toe." He grins. "Simple as that. Then I just slip on out and get the hell outta Dodge. Yeah!" Amused and impressed, Thelma calls him an outlaw. "Well, I may be an outlaw," he says, grinning at his own cheesiness, "but you're the one stealin' my heart." What follows is a night of sex so energetic that Thelma momentarily forgets her troubles.

She also takes leave of her senses. The following morning, she goes off to breakfast with Louise, leaving J.D. alone in the room with the money, and returns to find it stolen – a heartrending event that shatters the dregs of their optimism and leads directly to Thelma's first robbery, during which she repeats the young bandit's monologue virtually word-for-word. Soon after, the sensitive police inspector (Harvey Keitel) who's following the case gets J.D. alone in an interrogation room, smacks him upside the head with his own cowboy hat, and warns him that if anything happens to Thelma and Louise, he will be held "partly responsible." J.D. appears chastened. But as he's being led through the waiting area in handcuffs, he passes Thelma's husband and can't resist leering like a lech from an R. Crumb comic and murmuring, "Loooove your wife." The cuckolded hubby explodes with hapless rage. J.D. rubs it in by swiveling his pelvis suggestively.

Pitt had only 14 minutes of screen time in "Thelma and Louise," but they turned millions of heads. The attention showered on him went beyond his charisma and looks. Much was made of J.D.'s function in the movie's narrative, and rightly so; charming as the character is, he is ultimately no better, morally, than the man who tries to rape Thelma at the roadhouse. Both men are violators; J.D. is just more polite. Some critics also seized on the motel room tryst as proof of the plot's implausibility. Why, they asked, would a woman who has narrowly avoided sexual assault a day earlier invite a stranger into her bed, much less a hitchhiker? And why would she let him stay there after he reveals that he's served time for armed robbery? An article in *Time* pointed out that the scene itself reveled in precisely the kind of sexist movie clichés Callie Khouri's script was supposedly written to counter; it told audiences, in effect, that there is no female misfortune so vexing that can't be solved with a good lay. "How could Thelma – beaten and saved from a rape attempt by a murder at close range – beg to pick up a hitchhiker 18 hours later because she likes the cut of his jeans?" asked *Los Angeles Times* critic Sheila Benson. "To write such perky bounce-back doesn't suggest resilience, it suggests that no one's home emotionally." These complaints didn't stick, because "Thelma and Louise" had become a bona fide pop culture phenomenon, raking in box office dollars; provoking heated discussions between couples across America; generating an endless stream of newspaper editorials (some outraged, some approving); inspiring a flood of tie-in artifacts, from fanzines to T-shirts to bumper stickers ("Thelma and Louise live!"); and grabbing a fistful of Oscar nominations the following spring, including best direction, best original script, and two best actress nominations for its leading ladies. (Only Khouri took home a statuette.)

The movie's success helped the careers of everyone associated

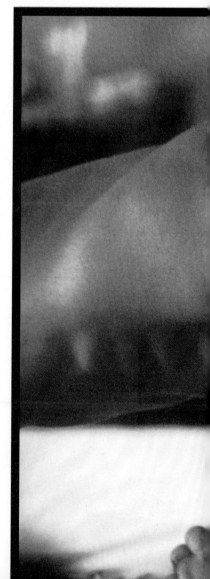

with it, but none more visibly than Pitt, who strode out of the film tagged as a smoldering hunk who could always find work as a model if the acting thing didn't pan out. To his chagrin, the tabloids linked him romantically with Geena Davis. And if he earned a dollar for every time a newspaper or magazine called him "the next James Dean," he could have retired wealthy without ever setting foot on a film set again.

Pitt's next two projects, "Cool World" and "Johnny Suede" – released a month apart in the summer of 1992, one full year after his breakthrough in "Thelma and Louise" – confounded the expectations of both moviegoers and the press. The first is a studio picture with a sizable budget, directed by Ralph Bakshi, a risqué ani-

mator who gained fame as a muckraking satirist in the '70s; the other is a surreal independent movie by a first-time director, with humor so dry it's parched.

An unmitigated disaster, "Cool World" follows an animator (Gabriel Byrne) into the two-dimensional world he created – a grotesque, decaying metropolis similar to the ones featured in previous Bakshi productions, including "Heavy Traffic" and "Fritz the Cat." Part live-action and

Continued on page 28

The "big break" came in the part of J.D. opposite Geena Davis in "Thelma and Louise." Subsequent tabloid reports romantically linking the two were predictable, given their on-screen chemistry.

21

Geena Davis

b. *Wareham, Massachusetts, 1957.* **"Thelma and Louise"** (1991). Geena Davis is one of those rare talents that command attention no matter how tiny the part. She turned heads in the small role of April in "Tootsie" (1982), and a short six years later was a surprise Academy Award winner as Best Supporting Actress in "The Accidental Tourist." She has since received two Golden Globe nominations for "A League of Their Own" and "Speechless" and an Oscar nomination for "Thelma and Louise."

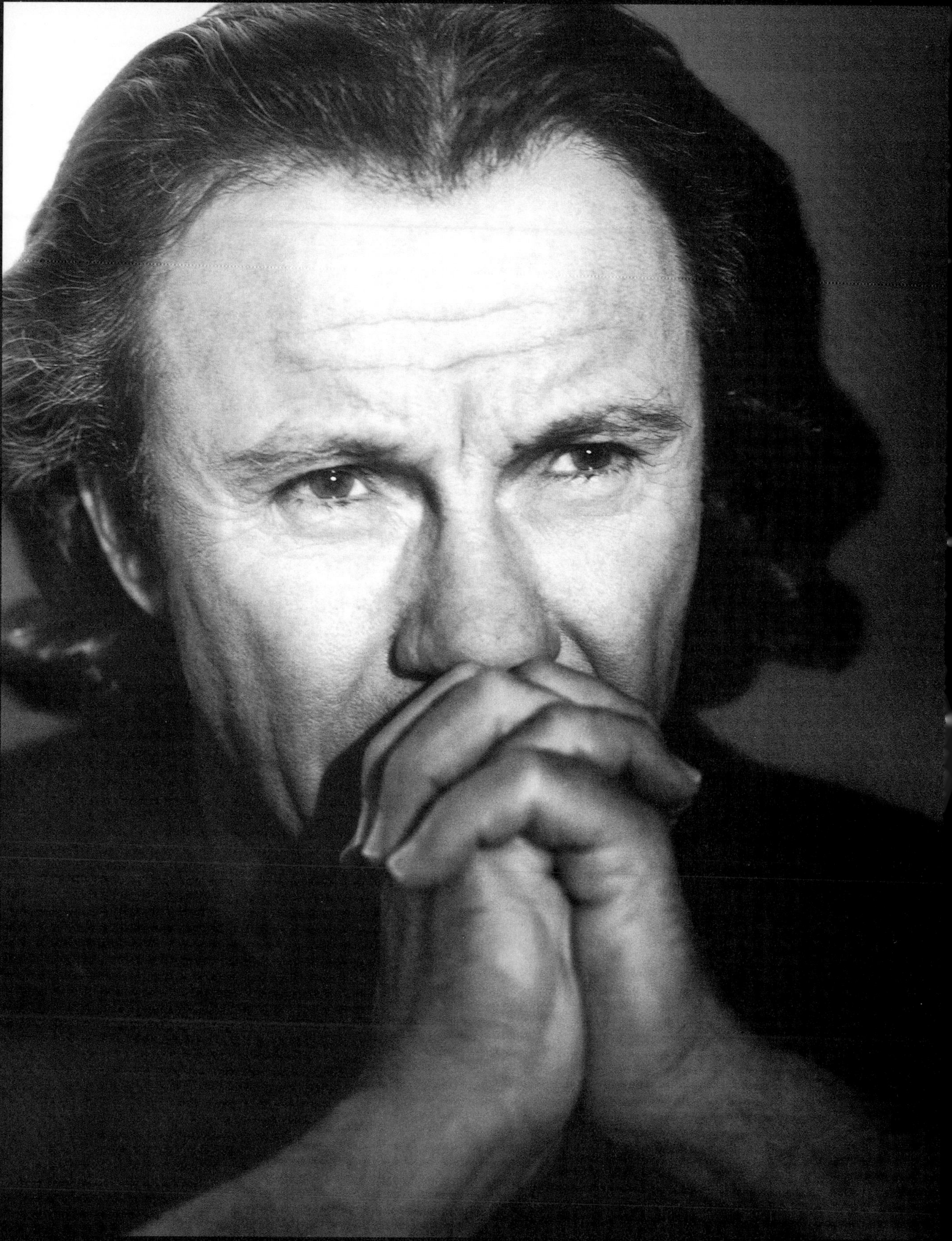

HARVEY

b. Brooklyn, New York, 1939. **"Thelma and Louise"** (1991). Harvey Keitel has spent virtually his entire career in the shadow of Robert De Niro. Even as the central figure in Martin Scorsese's "Mean Streets" (1973), Keitel was reduced to reacting to De Niro's histrionics. He is the consummate supporting player: always excellent, sometimes nominated, never crowned.

KEITEL

Val

b. Los Angeles, California, 1959. **"True Romance"** (1993). Val Kilmer is Brad Pitt with poor career choices. Although one of the youngest drama students ever admitted to Julliard, Kilmer spent eight long years as an actor before ever playing a part that required more of him than memorizing his lines. Even after his opinion-changing role as Jim Morrison in "The Doors," Kilmer frittered away any momentum as Elvis/Mentor in "True Romance" and Doc Holliday in the dreadful "Tombstone." He's since retreated into safe box office in "Batman Forever" and "The Saint."

KILMER

Pitt's insightful take on the character rescues the film from preciousness.

Continued from page 21

part animation, the film occasionally troubled itself to comment on the relationship between art and artist and the symbiotic link between fantasy and reality. Bakshi, who had been out of the feature film business for over a decade, hoped it would rejuvenate adult cartoons in America and revive his career, and even agreed to stay within the boundaries of the PG-13 rating to reach a wider audience. But his enthusiasm yielded nothing of interest. The project as a whole was so dull, poorly animated, and crudely conceived (complete with warty, gibbering goblins standing in for ethnic minorities, and a glorified guest shot by Kim Basinger as an animated party doll) that even the filmmaker's diehard fans loathed it.

As a human who has crossed over into Cool World and found work as a hipster detective, Pitt spent much of the movie standing around in a hepcat suit looking confused and impatient, which isn't surprising; he was given no character to play and no script to speak of, and found himself acting in front of bluescreens much of the time, struggling to envision cartoon splendors that wouldn't be created until long after he'd moved on.

"Johnny Suede" proved more interesting. Although it popped without warning into a handful of major cities in August 1992 and disappeared shortly after, it illustrates the actor's willingness to subvert his own beauty to take risks as an actor. Tom DiCillo, a cinematographer best known for his work with indie hipster filmmaker Jim Jarmusch ("Stranger than Paradise," "Mystery Train"), wrote and directed the surreal fable. Set "in the not too distant future," it concerns the life of the title character, an anonymous would-be pop star who idolizes Ricky Nelson, fancies himself a great lover, and wears his hair in a foot-high pompadour. The character of Johnny Suede is really just an extended actor's riff, and his "story" amounts to a gentle-spirited joke on viewers; his ambitions are slight, his talents virtually nonexistent, and his adventures deliberately uneventful and uninteresting. He falls in and out of love, tries to get a band together (it includes a brief appearance by Samuel L. Jackson as a bassist in a beret), dotes on a pair of velvet shoes he's convinced will fill the void in his life, and wanders around DiCillo's desolate urban panoramas looking sad, comical and clueless, like Sal Mineo in a Jerry Lee Lewis toupee. And that's pretty much it.

Pitt's insightful take on the character rescues the film from preciousness. He plays Johnny's narcissism and thickheaded confidence with an utterly straight face, so that his pompous speeches about music and love and his repeated assertions of his own uniqueness never become grating. He clearly loves being photographed unflatteringly. In one sequence, he paces around his cramped apartment clad only in a pair of dirty jockey shorts, muttering and fidgeting and scratching himself, then cuts a loud, apparently very satisfying fart just as a visitor comes calling; panicked, he waves his hands in the air, struggling to dispel the odor. The funniest scene in the film comes at Johnny's expense; in bed with a somewhat cynical date (Pitt's longtime friend Catherine Keener), he climaxes on top of her, then rolls over immediately and prepares to go to sleep. Indignant, the woman patiently explains to him that she'd like an orgasm too, please, if it's not too much trouble – a request that appears to surprise and astonish Johnny. She shows him how to get her off with his hand, a technique he has apparently never tried before. "It feels like you're trying to pick up a

When Pitt strikes a pose, it's easy to understand the early comparisons to James Dean, particularly considering his breakthrough role as J.D.

watermelon seed," she tells him.

The first years of stardom were both satisfying and dizzying to Pitt. He was enjoying his relationship with Juliette Lewis, who shared his absurdist sense of humor and urge to stretch as an actor, and he was being courted for leading roles on the strength of his work in "Thelma and Louise." But he was also being pursued sporadically by the tabloid press and plastered all over the pages of teen magazines. For every person who thought of him as an heir to the tradition of Marlon Brando, Paul Newman, and James Dean, there was another who dismissed him as the male Farrah Fawcett of the '90s.

The situation would become more vexing after his next major film, Robert Redford's 1920s melodrama "A River Runs Through It," an intel-

ligent and serious film that nonetheless treated him more as a symbol than a person. Based on the autobiographical novel by Norman MacLean, who died at 86 before the film was completed, the movie is a gentle-spirited meditation on family, nature, responsibility and fate. The main characters are two handsome siblings: Norman (Craig Sheffer), a book-smart fellow who wants to leave his small Montana town for a career teaching college in a big city; and Paul (Pitt), his roguishly charming but reckless younger brother. They learn about God, loyalty, and fly-fishing from their stern Methodist father (Tom Skerritt), find love, and take different paths in life. The story is told through Norman's eyes (with narration by Redford himself), which necessarily limits the audience's insight into the demons that drive Paul. We learn that Norman envies Paul's effortless fly fishing skill, his serenity, and his ability to be satisfied with life's simple pleasures; but he

"Johnny Suede" proved Pitt's willingness to step outside his looks to play with the "hunk" image.

doesn't understand his dark side. Paul is a hard drinker and has a temper (though it's often deployed to defend people weaker than himself). From his choice of girlfriend (an Indian, considered off-limits by the town's white populace) to his indifference towards paying off massive gambling debts, he seems to take pride in making everything in his life as difficult as possible.

Pitt had wanted the part badly every since he heard about the project in the summer of 1991. He tracked the picture's progress in Hollywood trade papers and read MacClean's novella obsessively, and when he finally auditioned for Redford, he was overcome with nervousness. Convinced he'd blown it, he asked a group of friends to help him tape a second audition at home. "Johnny Suede" co-star Catherine Keener made period costumes for Pitt. Her husband, actor Dermot Mulroney, shot it on video. Rocker Melissa Ethridge strummed her guitar in the background to provide musical ambiance. Pitt took the cassette to Redford and asked him to please take another look. Redford would later say that what sold him on Pitt wasn't the actor's auditions; it was the mix of toughness and sensitivity he exuded in casual conversation. He liked Pitt from the start.

Shooting took place in and around Bozeman, Montana, against spectacular mountain backdrops. Pitt was awed at first by the presence of Redford. "Butch Cassidy and the Sundance Kid" was the first movie he remember seeing as a child. He fondly recalled watching the actor's

The only outright disaster for Pitt was "Cool World," in which he played a detective with nothing to do, nothing to say, and no one to say it to.

movies at the drive-in as a young man, and admired Redford's intellectual honesty and effortless confidence both as a movie star and a filmmaker.

"You know when you play tennis with someone better than you, how your game gets better?" Pitt said. "That's how it became. He's just an all-around good man." Pitt also professed an affinity for the movie's grand theme: the ties that bind a family together. "I think for anyone who places any kind of importance in family and who maybe has a brother, I don't see how it can't hit you."

Pitt won favorable reviews, as did the film itself, which performed surprisingly well at the box office despite its restrained style and downbeat ending. And the way it feasted on Pitt's chiseled face, lanky body, and blond hair was at one with the film's awed view of Montana's scenic beauty. Redford and his cinematographer, Phillippe Rousselot, hype Pitt's handsomeness with nearly homoerotic obsessiveness. He is often seen posed against sparkling bodies of water, or looming heroically against preternaturally blue skies; sometimes, when the sunlight strikes the pollen swirling through the air at just the right angle, he seems to have his very own halo. Many

Craig Sheffer gave "A River Runs Through It" its point-of-view, but Pitt gave it its vibrancy.

reviewers speculated that the film's director idealized Pitt because he saw in him an image of his own youthful cockiness and beauty. Profiles of the actor began substituting the phrase "the next James Dean" with "the next Robert Redford."

Redford rose to Pitt's defense whenever reporters brought up the comparison, insisting the younger man be described on his own terms and praising Pitt's low-key performance.

Later, though, Pitt would tell reporters that the film's structure – and the understandable jitters that accompanied working for a childhood movie hero and Oscar-winning director – sometimes made him feel boxed in. He didn't like his own work in the movie. "My performance on 'A River Runs Through It' was weak," he told *Newsday* three years later. "I was just bad. . . . I felt this pressure not to let Redford down, and ultimately that gets in the way. So what do you learn? Just do your thing."

Pitt's follow-up took him light years away from Redford's sun-kissed rural poetry. Shot in 1992 before the release of "A River Runs Through It," "Kalifornia" was another movie about innocents encountering corruption and depravity while traveling the interstates in a

Intimidated by the presence of Redford, whose "Butch Cassidy and the Sundance Kid" was the first film he remembered seeing, Pitt felt his work on "A River Runs Through It" was lacking.

gas-guzzling convertible (a movie subgenre vast enough to merit its very own wall at Blockbuster). But the tone and subject matter were a lot grimmer, the script less accessible to mainstream crowds. It would become the second and last collaboration between Pitt and longtime girlfriend Juliette Lewis, who would break up soon afterward.

Written by Tim Metcalfe (best known for "Revenge of the Nerds") and directed by first-time feature filmmaker Dominic Sena, a razzle-dazzle stylist weaned on TV commercials and music videos, the movie was a moral fable about a couple of high-minded yuppie sophisticates (Michelle Forbes and David Duchovny,

future star of Fox TV's "The X-Files") who drive across America researching a book on famous mass murder sites. To cut costs, they post a notice asking for a second couple to come along and share expenses.

Unfortunately, the ad is answered by Early Grayce (Pitt) and Adele Corners (Lewis), a pair of dirt poor trailer park lovers so dimwitted, grotesque, and perverse that they could be Max Cady's long lost children. She is a meek woman-child whose fluttery gestures and archaic slang suggest Geraldine Page reincarnated as a Deep South mall rat; he's a paroled murderer with a cocky walk, a dirty beard, Neanderthal ideas about relationships, and a propensity to solve every problem he encounters, no matter how minor, by killing somebody. (He's like J.D.'s bigger, badder, uglier older brother.) The script wove navel-gazing academic platitudes about the meaning of murder around a rather transparent irony: two sensitive liberals morbidly fascinated by killers end up inviting one along for a cross-country ride.

On first glance, Pitt and Lewis appear to give irritatingly mannered performances. They deliver their lines with carefully studied earnest ignorance, repeating certain physical and vocal tics so ritualistically that it seems unthinkable that Brian and Carrie would put up with them long enough to discover their true natures. Their exis-

Continued on page 42   **33**

ROBERT

b. Santa Monica, California, 1937. **"A River Runs Through It"** (1992). The Pitt/Redford comparisons spewed from every source following the debut of "A River Runs Through It," but Redford has more in common with Tom Cruise than with Pitt. Like Cruise, Redford stays within well-defined emotional walls. Not surprisingly, Redford has been honored more often as a director (winning an Oscar for "Ordinary People" and a nomination for "Quiz Show") than as an actor ("The Sting").

REDFORD

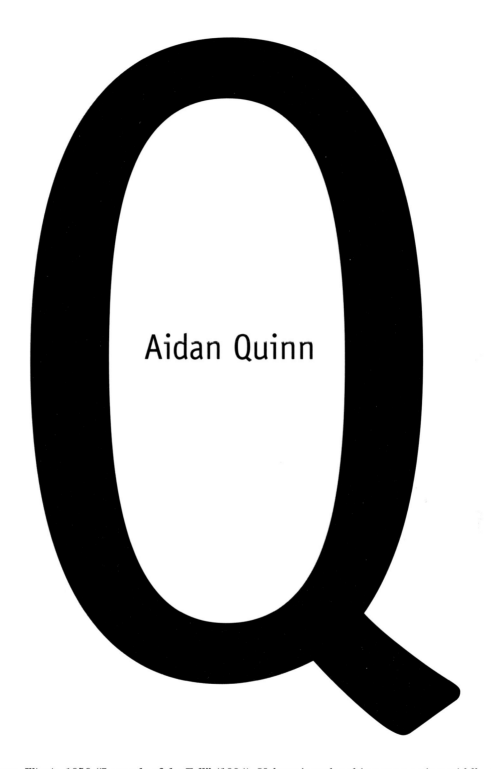

Aidan Quinn

b. Chicago, Illinois, 1959. **"Legends of the Fall"** (1994). If there is such a thing as an acting middle class, Aidan Quinn is its spokesman: good-looking, the right age, competent at his craft — but forever lacking the hook that would lift him off the treadmill of small films and second-banana parts. **37**

TOM CRUISE

b. *Syracuse, New York, 1962.* **"Interview with the Vampire"** (1994). The polar opposite of Pitt in temperament and style, Cruise nevertheless is Pitt's closest rival in ability and appeal. Compare his career trajectory to that of his equally fresh-faced contemporaries in the stellar cast of Francis Ford Coppola's "The Outsiders" (C. Thomas Howell, Ralph Macchio, Matt Dillon, Rob Lowe, Patrick Swayze, Emilio Estevez) in 1983, and Cruise's impact becomes even more clear.

Bruce

WILLIS

b. Germany, 1955. **"Twelve Monkeys"** (1995). No one ever questioned Bruce Willis' flair for comic banter or his ability to wring every last buck out of a sequel, but nearly everyone questioned his acting until "Pulp Fiction" and then "Twelve Monkeys" came along. With the right part and the right script, he could become the first in his family to garner an Academy Award nomination. (Demi, are you listening?)

Pitt and Lewis are resourceful actors playing limited people

Continued from page 33
tence simply doesn't mesh with the polished, easygoing professionalism of their co-stars – or, for that matter, with Sena's direction, which falls squarely in the perfume-commercial-with-blood style perfected by Ridley Scott and his brother Tony ("The Hunger," "True Romance").

Subsequent viewings yield a different opinion. The film is so predictable in its structure, so pointlessly glossy in its look and sound, and so humorless in the way it makes certain obvious points over and over (killing isn't just an abstract idea, even pacifists will commit murder to protect themselves, there are evil people out there who can't be explained with academic theories, etc., etc.) that Pitt and Lewis become objects of fascination rather than loathing. Adele isn't deluded when she defends her boyfriend; she simply doesn't know the horrors he's capable of committing, and she continues to see a potential for goodness in him that vanished long ago.

And though Early may not be book smart, it's obvious that, like Stanley Kowalski in "A Streetcar Named Desire," he has a certain animal cunning. He can spot other people's weaknesses and rub them raw, and he can strategically overplay the brawny, ignorant hick to put Brian and Carrie on the defensive. It is also clear that on some deep level, Adele and Early truly do love each other; not even the death of one at the other's hands can change that. Simultaneously more basic and more complicated than the movie they appear in, they disrupt Sena's slick visuals and Metcalfe's overly schematic screenplay with bursts of genuine crudity, desperation and ugliness, scuttling across the picture's MTV surface like cockroaches fouling a rich man's kitchen.

Seen through this prism, Pitt and Lewis aren't misguided actors giving limited performances. They are, instead, resourceful actors playing limited people with a dedication that borders on fanaticism. The moviemakers simply can't figure Early and Adele out; and so, like Brian and Carrie, they underestimate and patronize them. That "Kalifornia" is of interest today only because of Pitt and Lewis' involvement with it amounts to

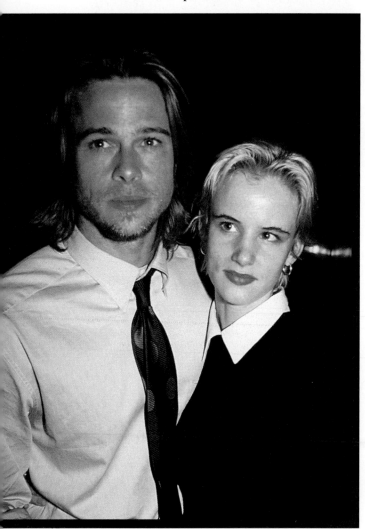

Pitt and Lewis arrive together at the premiere of "A River Runs Through It." Prior to the film, he walked the streets unrecognized. Afterward, the paparazzi chronicled his every move.

with a dedication that borders on fanaticism.

In "True Romance" Pitt played a small part as a stoner so zoned out he got a laugh out of hit men barging into his apartment. The film is notable only because of the Quentin Tarantino script.

the low-rent lovers' long-delayed revenge.

"Kalifornia" was not a financial success, mainly because it was too arty and too brutal to lure the dating crowd, not to mention borderline impossible to promote. (Some theater owners refused to book it because of its violence.) But it did win a few critical champions (including *Chicago Sun-Times* critic Roger Ebert, who put it on his year end Top Ten list) and drew renewed attention to Pitt, who was fast establishing himself as not just another pretty face. "Kalifornia" came out in

spring 1993, around the same time as "True Romance," another violent road movie about underclass lovers on the run. Written by a then-cult figure named Quentin Tarantino and directed by master hype artist Tony Scott, its cast included Pitt in a small part as a giggling stoner so detached from reality that he greets a pair of hitmen invading his home with befuddled politeness and amusement.

By the middle of 1993, Pitt had become firmly ensconced in the Hollywood scene. He had broken up with Lewis, a subject he would refuse to discuss in the future; all he would say was that they remained friends. "She's from another planet, but a good planet," he told *Cosmopolitan.* He was subsequently linked to a number of

The pairing of Cruise and Pitt drew so much attention that *Entertainment Weekly* went so far as to publish an interview with teen-age co-star Kirsten Dunst on which man was the better kisser. (She nominated Pitt for the honor.)

women, mostly actresses, none of whom stayed in his life very long. He told reporters that his partying phase downshifted considerably after the death of his friend River Phoenix, who collapsed outside the Viper Room in Los Angeles from a drug overdose. "Listen, you experiment around in different ways, but I know the truth about drugs," he told the Chicago Sun-Times. "People either quit or they die. I believe in learning from others' mistakes."

Edging towards 30, he had traded his devil-may-care image for a more domestic one. He was looking into buying homes in Los Angeles and in the Ozark mountains near his Missouri hometown, and he'd developed a taste for expensive antique furniture. High-profile film offers poured in with increasing frequency, but he was trying to be choosy. He took a small part as a bright, handsome artist who loved Elizabeth McGovern in the offbeat romantic comedy "The Favor," and cast about for a film that would make him an undisputed superstar.

He found it when Neil Jordan cast him in Anne Rice's supernatural epic "Interview with the Vampire." It was the subject of more pre-release speculation than any book-to-movie production since "Bonfire of the Vanities." Like that bestseller,

Rice's book had sold millions of copies worldwide and was the object of cultlike fascination. Since its paperback publication in the late 1970s, fans the world over had speculated on who could best play the two main characters: Louis, the troubled narrator who is robbed of his humanity against his wishes; and Lestat, the foppish undead prince who made him a vampire. Most of the talk focused on Lestat, the more flamboyant of the two characters. Even Rice joined the fray, suggesting Rutger Hauer in the early '80s, then switching her allegiance to rocker and actor Sting, a fan of the novelist whose stage presence served as inspiration for the 1985 sequel "The Vampire Lestat," in which the antihero had become a pop star. (He repaid the compliment by putting a Rice-inspired lament, "Moon Over Bourbon Street," on his 1987 album "Dream of the Blue Turtles.") By the early '90s, the public's wish list often mentioned Irish-born Method actor Daniel Day-Lewis, with the role of Louis earmarked for pint-sized Shakespearean wunderkind Kenneth Branagh.

When Warner Bros. finally shifted the project into "go" mode and announced its final casting choices, Rice devotees reacted like vampires plunged into holy water: Megastar Tom Cruise had claimed the role of Lestat. Although he'd won respect as an actor in critically acclaimed hits such as "Born on the Fourth of July" and "Rain Man," he was still perceived as an All-American hunk with a blindingly cocky grin. And Pitt, best known to the public for his golden boy parts in "Thelma and Louise" and "A River Runs Through It," would play Louis. The very idea of two actors viewed primarily as sex symbols playing such dark and complicated roles seemed the height of heresy to Rice fans. Even the author was appalled; she said casting Tom Cruise as Lestat was about as appropriate as letting Edward G. Robinson play Rhett Butler.

Filming commenced that fall in San Francisco,

New Orleans and Paris. The script was moderately faithful to the book, in structure if not spirit. The story of Louis' plunge into eternal damnation is cast as an extended flashback told to an inquisitive mortal interviewer (Christian Slater, replacing River Phoenix, who died shortly before shooting started). Jordan, who was then coming off the Oscar-nominated mystery thriller "The Crying Game," approached the material with his usual fluid camerawork, attention to detail and sympathy for society's outsiders, finding a hushed, dreamy, elegant tone that made the tale's sudden explosions of graphic violence all the more startling.

The shoot was far from uneventful. Expensive on-location footage from New Orleans proved

Pitt retained his vampirish appearance long enough after the cameras stopped rolling to attend the premiere of the film with the proper look.

Pitt doesn't talk much about his role in "Vampire", and it's not difficult to imagine why . . .

unusable and had to be reshot at great expense, and the media seemed more interested in the spat between Rice and Warner Bros. – and the public's skepticism about Cruise as Lestat – than in the movie itself. To make matters worse, articles began appearing in alternative newspapers and in the gay and lesbian press claiming the novel's provocative sexual underpinnings were being played down. The alleged culprit was Cruise, who had battled rumors of repressed homosexuality throughout his career in Hollywood. Media reports said Cruise was

uncomfortable with Lestat's pan-sexual appetites and insisted on script rewrites to make the character more obviously straight.

This provoked an outcry. Rice's work was anything but reactionary. Her fiction was about transgression – about stepping beyond the boundaries of acceptable behavior, then learning to live as an outsider without guilt or shame. She turned Bram Stoker's Victorian-era skittishness about sexuality inside-out and made the monsters the heroes. Unlike Count Dracula and the creatures from Stephen King's "Salem's Lot,"

... He was stuck in the same hapless narrator role as Craig Sheffer in "A River Runs Through It."

who were depicted as emissaries of darkness who had to be destroyed for the greater good of society, Lestat and company weren't figures of pure evil. They were complex individuals who just happened to feast on the flesh of the living, and they'd managed to construct an elaborate worldwide subculture that allowed vampires to live and thrive despite the persecutions of mortals. They were portrayed as an essential and permanent part of human civilization.

Rice always had a huge gay and lesbian readership for precisely this reason. Her novels were part of a long tradition of pop culture works that turned worst case stereotypes inside out and made them empowering, even liberating. "Thelma and Louise" addressed real issues of heterosexual relationships in a mythic context; blaxploitation movies of the early 1970s pulled off the same trick, building politically charged storylines around pimps, prostitutes, studs, hustlers and other stereotypes. In the same vein, Rice's vampire books can be read as fantastic tall tales about a homosexual underground that has existed throughout history. Cruise and Jordan professed to understand this, were annoyed by accusations that they didn't, and used the media to reassure Rice devotees that they weren't defiling the novel. The skepticism persisted. (At this stage of the game, Pitt wasn't often quoted on the subject, mostly because he was third on the project's celebrity totem pole, behind the star and the director.)

The finished product, released November 15, 1994, grossed a record-breaking $45 million in its first five days. But its reception was rocky. Controversy-stoking talk show hosts complained about the film's excessive bloodletting; some

The relaxed Pitt and the driven Cruise butted heads often on the set of "Interview with the Vampire." Not only did their styles clash, an unspoken rivalry constantly hung in the air between them.

Rice fans griped that the lead characters' pansexuality had indeed been watered down; and reviewers and ticket buyers either liked the film and loathed the stars or vice-versa.

Cruise reveled in all the attention about his career choice, which was described as "risky," probably because despite concessions to his superstar image, Lestat was still a perverse, sadistic and profoundly unlikable character. When a writer from *Vanity Fair* told Cruise that he'd played Lestat as "a bitch god," the star chuckled approvingly. Perhaps he understood that there was only so much that could be done to tame a project like "Vampire"; when you play a dashing, dandyish nightcrawler who dresses like Prince and talks like an Oscar Wilde hero, subtext has a way of coming through no matter what. And in any case, the film's financial success made the point moot. Even Anne Rice experienced an eleventh hour change of heart; a week before "Vampire" opened, she purchased a two-page ad in *The New York Times* to relay her newfound confidence in Cruise, Pitt, Jordan and the movie.

Pitt doesn't talk much about his role in "Vampire" these days, and it's not difficult to imagine why. He was stuck in the same hapless narrator role as Craig Sheffer in "A River Runs Through It," reacting against an antagonist who's stronger, sexier, and worst of all, funnier than he is. Louis comes off as listless and dull-witted, an exasperating stick-in-the-mud who pores over the same basic moral qualms for literally hundreds of years without ever coming to terms with them. Pitt seems stymied by the very thought of playing him and withdraws into a sleepy, disinterested fog, and for the first time in his career, he's boring to watch. He even reads the film's voice-over in a monotone so flat that Kevin Costner's narration in "Dances With Wolves" sounds joyous in comparison. (Louis is a nerdy worrywart in the

Tristan is both active and passive, adoring and adored — the ideal superhero for the New Age '90s.

book, too, but he's also quick-witted and introspective, and he tells his sad tale with gusto.)

Pitt's performance perks up only when he dotes on his surrogate daughter, Claudia (Kirsten Dunst), a little girl treated as a snack by Louis, then thoughtlessly transformed into a vampire by Lestat. Louis feels both tenderness and intense guilt towards Claudia, and their affection for each other is the only credible relationship in sight. Unfortunately, by the film's final act both Lestat and Claudia have vanished; audience interest soon follows.

The idea of spending an eternity with Louis is as appetizing as a lukewarm cup of blood. It's tough to envision how even Louis could stand it, which may explain why the film's final scene unintentionally drew laughter from some viewers. After Louis ends his story and flees before the rising of the sun, Lestat pops up unexpectedly in the interviewer's car, kills him, and listens to Louis' recorded interview for about 10 seconds before ejecting it from the cassette player. "Can you imagine listening to that for two centuries?" he demands. The answer is no; two hours is quite enough. Pitt conceded as much in a 1995 *Chicago Sun-Times* interview.

"Listen, this Louis guy is such a drag," he said. "He's depressed. From beginning to end. Six months, six days a week . . . And it's hard to look at Tom Cruise and say lines like, 'I'll see you in hell.' It gets to you."

He also confirmed rumors that he and Cruise clashed on the set. While Pitt was famed for his laid-back manner, Cruise was a notoriously hard-driving detail man. "Tom's very precise," Pitt told *Cosmopolitan*. "I always thought there was this underlying competition that got in the way of any real conversation. Tom's North Pole and I'm South."

No matter: "Interview with the Vampire" went on to become the biggest box office success of Pitt's career, pulling in $200 million worldwide. Perhaps this indicated that moviegoers had more faith in Jordan's casting than critics did. Then again, it may have simply confirmed the suspicion that with aggressive marketing by a major Hollywood studio, there is no such thing as bad press. In any case, Pitt now occupied a plum position in Hollywood's casting hierarchy. The spectacular opening of "Vampire" created an unprecedented groundswell of public interest. Fan clubs sprouted like daffodils after a heavy rain, and columnists reported a sudden proliferation of Brad Pitt posters and photographs in student lockers and office cubicles across America.

Only a year earlier, while on location in Ontario shooting his next film, "Legends of the Fall," Pitt was able to walk down the street in most major American cities mostly unrecognized. Now he found himself accosted by panting, stammering autograph seekers everywhere he went. The tabloid press turned up the heat and made him the subject of an unending stream of blatantly untrue stories, from the soapy (He'd become involved with a married woman in Los Angeles and broken up her marriage) to the downright surreal (He'd donated sperm to Martians). Whenever coveted leading roles were discussed, his name was now mentioned in the same breath with Tom Cruise. His asking price hovered between $6 and $8 million per picture.

But there were still doubts that he could carry a whole film alone, without help from a celebrity director like Jordan or a superstar partner like Cruise. What he needed was a mainstream hit whose success would be credited solely to his drawing power – a project that would make him an icon.

That film was "Legends of the Fall," which opened in New York and Los Angeles within a month of "Vampire" and expanded nationwide in January 1995. Based on the novella by critically acclaimed tough guy writer Jim Harrison ("Revenge"), it had been in the works since 1992. Director Ed Zwick – a co-creator of the popular adult drama series "thirtysomething" and a film director with one successful movie, the Civil War epic "Glory," to his credit – had secured the rights many years earlier and had approached Pitt about starring in it while prints of "A River Runs Through It" were still wet from the lab. Pitt responded instantly to the film's outdoor spirit,

"Legends of the Fall" proved the perfect follow-up to "Vampire." As Tristan Ludlow, Pitt proved his ability to carry a film on his star-power alone.

domestic fireworks and quasi-religious overtones.

Set in Montana in the early part of the century, the story concerned the rising and falling fortunes of the Ludlow family, a colorful clan with a gruff patriarch (Anthony Hopkins) and three sons of radically different temperament. The eldest, Alfred (Aidan Quinn), is a book-smart fellow who will later find fame as a politician. The youngest, Samuel (Henry Thomas, the hero of "E.T.," all grown up at last) was idealistic, loyal, and naive. The troubled middle child, Tristan (Pitt), was a mysterious loner who seemed attuned to nature. Both stronger and more emotionally volatile than his brothers, he finds himself torn between protecting his fam-

49

ily and abandoning it for years at a stretch. When a beautiful woman named Susannah (Julia Ormond) arrives on the Ludlow property, she throws the family's dynamic hopelessly out of whack. The three brothers fight for her attention; over the next several years, she marries Samuel and loses him to World War I, then marries Alfred only to become disgusted with his unscrupulous political ambitions. The whole time, she carries a torch for Tristan.

So does "Legends of the Fall," which treats the character so reverently that the film's title could be placed in a dictionary next to the phrase "star

vehicle." Like Hawkeye in "Last of the Mohicans," Tristan is a pumped-up, long-haired sex god – an enigmatic force of nature who wrestles grizzlies, slices German soldiers' scalps off, breaks wild stallions, talks to the trees, sails the globe in search of spiritual counsel, and gets along swimmingly with every nonwhite person he meets (which, in movies, means that he's soul-

Pitt deliberately undermined his sex-symbol image in "Twelve Monkeys," wearing contacts that made him appeared cock-eyed and basing his mannerisms on personal observation of patients in an asylum.

ful). Even the film's narrator, One Stab (Gordon Tootoosis), a Native American whose wizened mind seems to contain all the secrets of the universe, professes to be incapable of fathoming his complexity. Zwick photographs Pitt like a cross between Rambo, Paul Bunyan, John Holmes, Gary Cooper and Jesus Christ; grants him not one, not two, but three long-distance entrances on horseback while James Horner's symphonic score swells like a baboon's hindquarters during estrus; and favors him with so many golden-hued close-ups that Ormond's function as love object is effectively obliterated. Tristan is both active and passive, masculine and feminine, adoring and adored – in short, the ideal superhero for the New Age '90s.

"**L**egends of the Fall," to its credit, knows exactly what kind of movie it is: an epic historical tearjerker designed to pander shamelessly to moviegoers of both genders while hyping its star as a smoldering, unreachable savior-stud. Pitt was clearly game for the part, and during a 1995 publicity tour selling the movie, his insistence that he was uncomfortable tapping into his own glamour rang hollow. After *People* named him "Sexiest Man Alive," Pitt jokingly claimed that the cover line had been misspelled. "It was supposed to be 'Sexiest Moron.' " He balked at renewed comparisons with James Dean and Robert Redford and even insisted that a February story in *Vanity Fair* had unfairly misrepresented him as the latest dish of beefcake. The cover shot showed Pitt clad in a puffy magician-style shirt and the same kind of leather pants he claimed to loathe during his "Dallas" days; wind whipped his hair and pushed his shirt open to expose one nipple. "I wanna know, who picked that picture?" he asked *Newsday* rhetorically. "Do they not like me? It's amazing to me, completely amazing." One won-

ders why Pitt didn't voice his objections while the *Vanity Fair* photo crew fitted him with gigolo clothes and wheeled in a gigantic fan.

To be fair, the actor did bring more to Tristan Ludlow than abs, glutes, and a big, manly beard. Pitt always said Tristan was the first part he felt certain he was born to play, and his carefully modulated performance bears this out. He works against the role's built-in capacity for silliness, leavening soapy romantic interludes with flashes of bitterness and skepticism, and plunging into battle with a pained expression which suggests that just because Tristan is good at killing doesn't mean he enjoys it. He understands that Tristan's strength and beauty make him sexy, but his hints of inner darkness make him real. In that sense, his work in "Legends" owes less to James Dean than to another Missouri-reared movie star, Steve McQueen – an unaffected tough guy who, in the words of critic and historian David Thomson, possessed "a remorseless honesty."

Pitt's only painful miscalculation occurs during Tristan's first conversation with Susannah. He takes a fat swig of milk, gets some on his upper lip, and keeps talking without wiping it away. It's the kind of transparent, showboatish trick that most actors outgrow after high school, yet Pitt insists on doing it in film after film. Not that the audience cared, of course; when he took that sip of milk, a million viewers in ten thousand darkened movie houses offered him a napkin.

All the sex symbol talk nearly obscured his palpable success as a leading man. The Hollywood Foreign Press association honored him with a Golden Globe nomination as Best Actor in a drama, and he was touted for an Academy Award in the same category. (He was not nominated; the film received one Oscar, for Best Cinematography.) Except for *Chicago Tribune* critic Gene Siskel, Pitt's acting abilities found few defenders in the press, which preferred to paint

Continued on page 58

Gwyneth Paltrow

b. 1972. **"Seven"** (1995). Paltrow's star-making turn in "Emma" finally erased the permanent parenthetical phrase "Brad Pitt's girlfriend" from every first reference to her in print, but she now enters that phase of career when comparisons are not only inevitable but mandatory. Perhaps the greatest line to come out of the post-"Emma" hype was that she had the sexiest neck since Audrey Hepburn.

MORGAN FREEMAN

b. Memphis, Tennessee, 1937.
"Seven" (1995). Despite the emphasis on youth in cinema, Morgan Freeman waited until the age of 50 to capture the public's attention, when he played a pimp in "Street Smart" (1987). He earned an Academy Award nomination for Best Support-ing Actor for that role, and followed with a Best Actor nomination for "Driving Miss Daisy" and a key supporting role in "Unforgiven," Oscar's Best Picture of 1992.

b. Chicago, Illinois, 1942. **"Devil's Own"** (1997). Possibly the all-time box-office champion, Ford's credits include three "Star Wars" films, three "Indiana Jones" films, "The Fugitive," "Witness," "Working Girl," "Blade Runner," "American Graffiti" — and yet he still seems a cipher as an actor. One can't help but wonder if he's been swimming or was just swept along by the George Lucas/ Steven Spielberg tidal wave that swelled underneath his career.

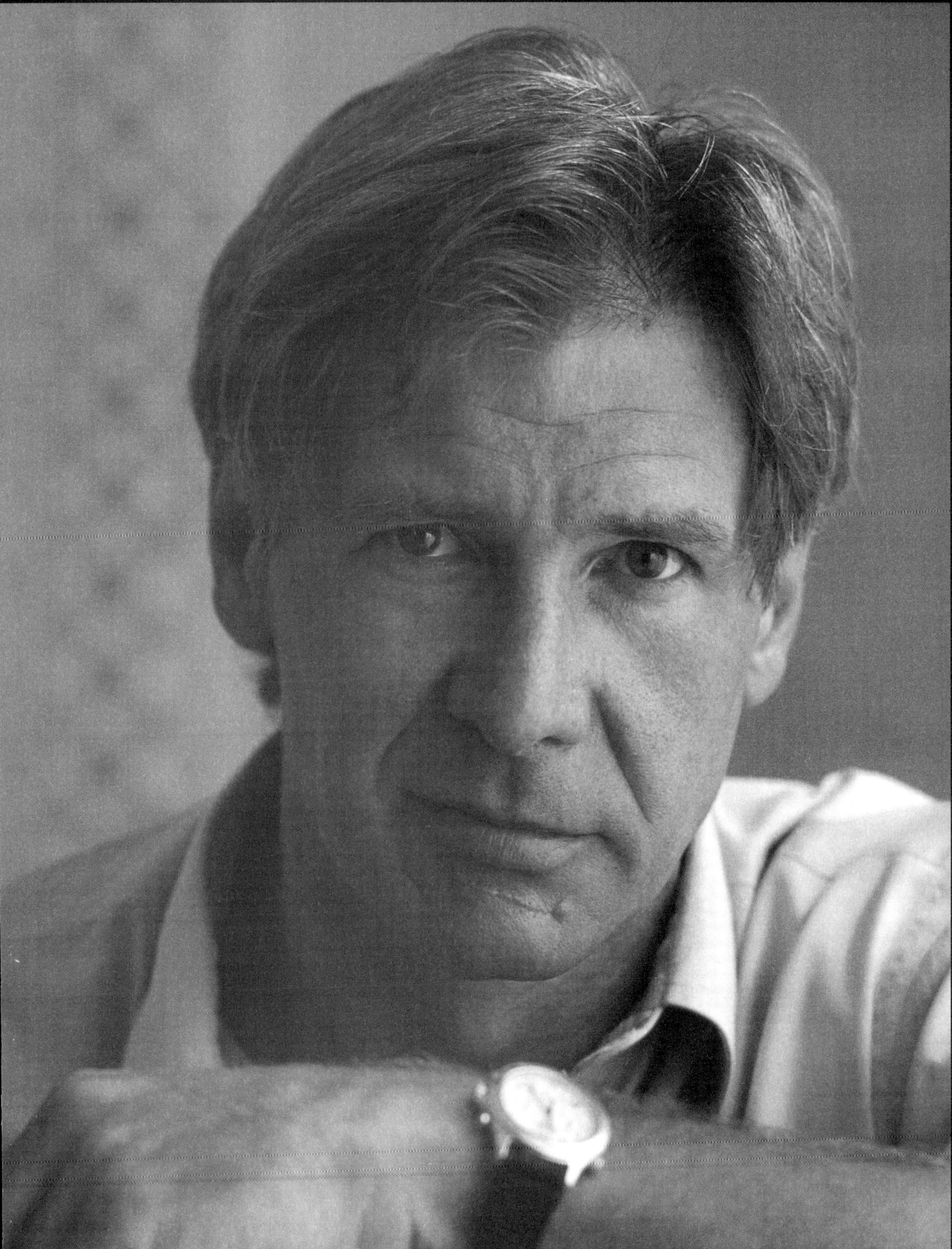

Continued from page 51
him as the latest model of male sexpot.

On those terms, Pitt already had entered the lexicon of popular culture. In the spring of 1995, the second film by "Johnny Suede" writer-director Tom DiCillo was released. A low-budget film about making a low-budget film, its cast of characters included a blond, hunky, and revoltingly narcissistic leading man named Chad Palomino, amusingly played by indie film actor James LeGros. (DiCillo repeatedly insisted the character wasn't based on Pitt, but nobody believed him.) Around the same time, in an episode of the ABC teen drama "My So-Called Life," a girl-friend of the show's heroine disclosed that she always felt more excited about sex after watching a Brad Pitt movie.

"I was with him in England for the premiere of 'Legends of the Fall,' " Zwick told *Cosmopolitan* the following year. "We got out of the car in Leicester Square, and there were ten thousand girls screaming like he was the Beatles."

Besides superstardom, Zwick's film wrought another change in Pitt's life: the presence of Gwyneth Paltrow. A willowy blond actress sired in a showbiz family (her mother is actress Blythe Danner and her father is TV producer Bruce Paltrow), she first caught Pitt's eye when she auditioned for Julia Ormond's part in "Legends of the Fall." She was marked as an up-and-coming star after her breakthrough role in 1993's "Flesh and Bone," a Texas film noir written and directed by Steve Kloves, who made a splashy debut a few years earlier with the musical melodrama "The Fabulous Baker Boys." Paltrow won raves as the inscrutable, sociopathic girlfriend of Roy Sweeney (James Caan), a smiling killer whose past deadly sins come back to haunt his emotionally withdrawn son (Dennis Quaid).

In contrast to Juliette Lewis, who rocketed to prominence at approximately the same time as Pitt (both "Thelma and Louise" and "Cape Fear" were released in 1991), Paltrow was not a star. Like many talented young actresses in the '90s, she found herself competing for a painfully small number of leading women's roles against several more established competitors, including Julia Roberts, Winona Ryder, and, unfortunately, Lewis. Yet Paltrow already had won respect within the industry and was being groomed to star in a big-budget costume epic based on Jane Austen's novel "Emma." She also had a captivating public persona – an open, humble, earthy quality that made her unthreatening even to Pitt's most possessive female fans. By fall of 1993, the two had become the subject of tabloid marriage rumors and paparazzi stalkings.

By the time the tidal wave of superstardom hit, Pitt already was shooting his follow-up to "Legends of the Fall," a serial killer picture called "Seven." Penned by first time feature screenwriter Andrew Kevin Walker, "Seven" was a moody, hypnotic hate letter to the modern city, about a brilliant psychopath known only as John Doe (Kevin Spacey) who kills one victim a day for seven days, each killing committed in the spirit of one of the Old Testament's seven deadly sins. Pitt played the role of Detective Mills, a young hotshot investigator just transferred in from a small town; he butts heads but eventually learns from an older and wiser mentor, Detective Somerset (Morgan Freeman). Pitt suggested Paltrow for the small but pivotal role of Tracy, Mills' beautiful young wife. "The Tracy character was so important because it's the only sunshine we have in the film," he said. "This is the feel-bad movie of '95."

Pitt wasn't kidding about the sunshine remark. The film's director was David Fincher, a veteran of MTV who specialized in glossy images of semi-futuristic decay; his big breakthrough was Madonna's video for "Express Yourself," a pastiche of Fritz Lang's "Metropolis" that showed the blond vamp lording it over a Russian Constructivist-looking industrial zone populated by muscular, sweat-slicked studs. He'd stumbled with his first foray into theatrical films, the third installment in the "Alien" series, which had unnerving atmosphere to burn but little narrative momentum.

Pitt claimed his first major award — a Golden Globe — for "Twelve Monkeys." He also received an Oscar nomination but lost out to "Seven" co-star Kevin Spacey, who won for "The Usual Suspects."

He turned out to be a perfect choice for "Seven." While shooting the picture in and around Los Angeles in the fall of 1994, Fincher pushed the script's comic book grottiness to bold extremes, suffocating his vaguely retro sets in foggy darkness and drenching almost every outdoor scene in torrential sheets of rain. The shoot took its toll on Pitt, who continued to perform many of his own stunts. During a lengthy chase sequence that required him to jump from one rain-slicked car hood to another, he slipped and fell headfirst through a rear windshield, cutting tendons and nerves in his left hand. Despite this mishap, the production was satisfying. He got to work closely with Paltrow and he bonded with Freeman, a character actor-turned-American institution who rocketed to movie stardom in middle age in the 1987 urban thriller "Street Smart." After the shoot, Pitt described Freeman's majestic aura as "Morganic," and said that he and Paltrow thought the elder actor was the real Sexiest Man Alive. Freeman returned Pitt's respect, describing him in subsequent interviews as an attentive and gifted actor with innate movie star charisma. "He's to the manor born," he said.

While Pitt's performance in the movie revealed his self-confidence as a movie star, it also cemented his reputation as a resourceful and ambitious actor. In contrast to the august and literate Somerset, Mills was a simple man with a

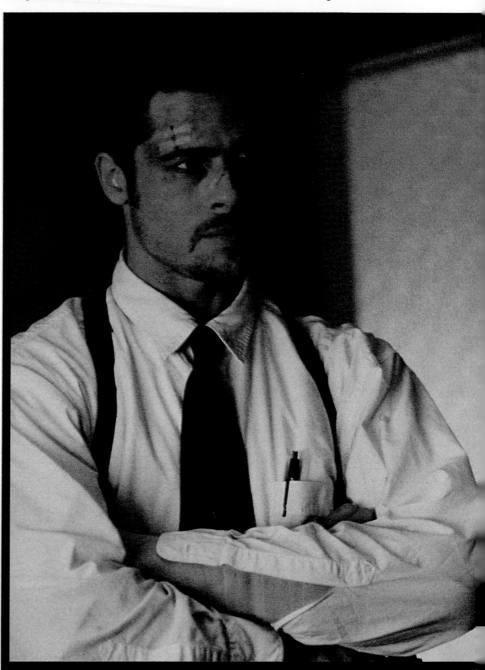

Brad has taken a leap that's going to amaze people. — "Twelve Monkeys" director Terry Gilliam.

short fuse, a cocky attitude towards police work, and a certain naiveté about the nature of evil. During the discovery of the film's first corpse, Pitt puts a slyly arch spin on the gallows wisecracks common to police thrillers, indicating that Mills is not so much a hardened investigator as a gifted newcomer who's watched too many cop shows on TV. He's not afraid to come off as thickheaded; in one memorable scene, he confidently mispronounces the Marquis de Sade's name so that it sounds like the soul singer's.

And his agonized expressions during the horrific finale reveal a clear understanding of Fincher and Walker's intentions. Granting the killer's request to be taken out into the desert, Mills and Somerset sight an express mail delivery van in the distance coming their way. The package it drops off contains the severed head of Mills wife. Before John Doe can even explain his intentions, Pitt's conflicted and powerful facial expressions – revulsion, grief, fear, rage – indicate that he already knows he's become a part of the killer's master plan, which requires the illustration of two more deadly sins. Doe, who says he covets the young detective's satisfying home life, is supposed to be "Envy," and has provoked Mills into becoming "Vengeance." He raises his arm and takes aim at Doe's head – gun hand shaking, tear-streaked face shifting between rational restraint and irrational anger, struggling to lower the pistol and avert his own tragic destiny. It was Pitt's finest two minutes of screen time.

Despite its relentless gore and downbeat finale, "Seven" was a surprise smash, grossing more than $100 million and showing up on a number of year-end critics' Top Ten lists. It was blasted in some corners for its bleak view of

Besides accolades for his growth as an actor, Pitt's role in "Seven" brought him more tangible rewards, as well — a head-first fall through a windshield while performing his own stunts.

humanity and was criticized for its near-pornographic images of corpses, but it was undeniably the product of a singular filmmaking consciousness; it had a look and feel like no other contemporary horror picture, which made even its routine buddy-cop and serial killer elements feel fresh. And in tone, it was miles away from the old-movie grandiosity of "Legends of the Fall," which was part of the reason Pitt chose "Seven" as his follow-up.

Still, the glamour factor lingered. Critical kudos aside, Pitt's magnetism was credited with making "Seven" a hit. When the film was released in fall 1995, the actor's new look – a buzz cut and a goatee – garnered nearly as much attention as the film itself.

"I'll be glad when people get used to it so the media can move onto other stories, like that little thing going on in Bosnia," Pitt responded. Nonetheless, he was pleased to have been a part of "Seven" and would describe the film as "the first step in what I call my 'killing Tristan Ludlow' period."

The next step involved stepping off center stage and taking a small part in an even stranger film, Terry Gilliam's "Twelve Monkeys," a time travel tale about a convict from the future who travels back to 1996 to uncover the roots of a virus that will eventually decimate humanity.

The stars of the piece were Bruce Willis, who played the time traveling James Cole, and Madeleine Stowe, cast as a contemporary psychiatrist who comes to believe in the time traveler's rants about impending plague. Pitt signed on for the supporting part of Jeffrey Goines, a spoiled rich boy raised by a scientific genius (Christopher Plummer) whose work involves experimentation on animals. A mentally unhinged individual, Goines is living in a

61

Philadelphia insane asylum at the start of the movie; he meets Cole, who has been briefly incarcerated there by police, and hears his stories about what life is like in the disease-ruined future. The stories inspire him to become a guerrilla activist; in rebellion against his father, he joins a secretive anti-animal-testing strike force known as the Army of the Twelve Monkeys. Like the "Terminator" and "Back to the Future" movies, Gilliam's film contains enough circular narrative elements to keep college students arguing all night, and Goines' predicament is at the center of it. The activists are believed to have caused the plague that destroyed humanity, yet Goines would never have been inspired to join and lead them if he hadn't met the time-traveling Cole.

To get in character, Pitt spent three weeks at Temple University hospital's psychiatric ward studying the mannerisms of insane people. When shooting began, he adopted his most severely unattractive look since Early Grayce in "Kalifornia." He alternated between unkempt short and long hair, always greasy, and was fitted with brown contact lenses, one of which was a false eyeball surface that made him look cock-eyed. The final nail in Tristan Ludlow's coffin was the performance itself. Pitt played the character as a babbling, hunched up, spastic goon, forever punctuating outlandish statements with Dennis Hopperish hand jabs and repeating certain phrases over and over like a mynah bird on amphetamines. Gilliam said Pitt saw his character as "a Charles Manson type" and based his mannerisms on people he met at the mental hospital.

"Brad was keen to do the part, one that was so unlike anything he'd tried before," Gilliam said. "He plays a fast-talking, wild, crazed person. I was intrigued by the idea, always like the idea, of casting against type. Brad has taken a leap, a dangerous leap, that's going to amaze people."

It didn't amaze everyone; in fact, when "Twelve Monkeys" was released in December 1995, critics and audiences were violently divided in their opinion of Pitt. Some reviewers praised him as a fearless and inventive actor, while others – including Terence Rafferty of The *New Yorker* – dismissed him as affected, annoying and simply

not credible. The sticking point was the deliberate artificiality of his performance. As radically different as they were in temperament and ambition, it wasn't hard to imagine Early Grayce, Paul McClean, Johnny Suede, and J.D. showing up at the same family picnic. Goines was different. He was a completely fantastic creation – a lunatic soothsayer, like the elfin homeless man played by Robin Williams in Gilliam's last movie, "The Fisher King," except hateful and violent.

By the time awards season rolled around the following spring, though, the consensus had tilted unequivocally in Pitt's favor. He won a Golden Globe as Best Supporting Actor in a drama and delivered a memorably crass acceptance speech that began, "I'd like to thank the makers of Kaopectate." And he was nominated for an Academy Award as Best Supporting Actor.

He lost to "Seven" co-star Kevin Spacey – who, coincidentally, was also nominated for playing a damaged, manipulative, gnomelike character, in Bryan Singer's convoluted crime drama "The Usual Suspects." But in a sense, Pitt triumphed anyway. Unlike Spacey, he was a proven box-office draw, which meant he could switch between Tristan Ludlows and Jeffrey Goineses and be reasonably confident that one type of film could subsidize the other. To top it off, he'd won a prize of more long lasting value than an Oscar: respect.

Pitt is in a unique position right now. With the exception of Harrison Ford, no A-list leading man has such a knack for picking projects that excite audiences without insulting their intelligence. He has consistently worked with directors who are intriguing artists, first-rate storytellers, or both: Ridley and Tony Scott, Robert Redford, Ralph Bakshi, Tom DiCillo, David Fincher, Ed Zwick, Neil Jordan, Terry Gilliam. And he stars in films that, with few exceptions,

work very effectively on their own terms. Sensitive domestic period dramas don't come much better than "A River Runs Through It." "Thelma and Louise" is the most emotionally resonant and politically relevant road picture since "Badlands." Science fiction doesn't get much classier than "Twelve Monkeys." "Seven" is a masterwork of grossout horror that would give Edgar Allan Poe the shivers. And if you're looking for an unapologetically sappy historical soap opera, "Legends of the Fall" will do the trick.

Recently, Pitt showed signs of settling into a career-maintenance mindset. In early 1996, he still was dating Gwyneth Paltrow but had shrugged off suggestions of impending marriage. He played a small but important role in Barry Levinson's epic urban drama "Sleepers," about a group of boys abused in reform school who take revenge against their tormentors as adults. He went on to spend seven months on location in New York City shooting Alan J. Pakula's cop drama "The Devil's Own," co-starring as a flamboyant IRA gunrunner who locks horns with stoic policeman Harrison Ford. Shooting dragged on for more than seven grueling months, and tabloids were filled with disturbing reports of egocentric clashes between Ford and Pitt, both of whom thought their character should be dominant in the story.

Time will bear out whether Pitt's micromanagement of his character will yield satisfying dramatic fruit, or if this is the first step towards the maintenance of a movie star image – a pursuit that, publicly, at least, he never seemed concerned with in the past.

When stars tell interviewers that the only opinions that count are those of average moviegoers, it's a sure sign of defensiveness. Loosely translated, that statement means, "I've taken a critical beating recently, so I've decided not to stray from the kinds of roles fans expect."

The most prominent exponent of this theory is Pitt's most famous contemporary, Tom Cruise. In 15 years of stardom, he has only strayed from his rigidly-defined screen persona twice, in "Born on the Fourth of July" and "Interview with the Vampire." In both films, he hardly could be said to have proven his detractors wrong; if he was, in fact, effective in those roles, it was partly due to the fact that his apple pie image lingered in the minds of ticket buyers. Those roles were the exceptions that proved the rule. One could measure the emotional distance between most of his other parts – "Rain Man," "Top Gun," "A Few Good Men," "The Firm" – in millimeters.

Pitt, in contrast, has yet to establish rules for himself. There is, as of this writing, no standard issue "Brad Pitt" character. Fans find him immensely appealing in romantic melodramas, and Pitt knows this and indulges their tastes by making those kinds of movies and posing for beefcake photos while promoting them; but when he chooses projects that don't fit the Paul MacLean/Tristan Ludlow mold, moviegoers accept him without prejudgment. The disturbing "Seven" grossed more in North America than his superstar vehicle "Legends of the Fall." And "Twelve Monkeys" – a violent, surreal, arty film so tortuously plotted that viewers needed a notepad to keep track of its twists and turns – grossed a surprising $60 million.

A more plausible explanation is this: Pitt has a knack for picking interesting scripts directed by interesting filmmakers that also happen to be entertaining. Some stars – Cruise, Arnold Schwarzenegger, Jim Carrey – appear in bigger hits, but their films often smack of obsessive packaging, tinkering and marketing. Other stars – notably Alec Baldwin, Denzel Washington, Johnny Depp and Nicolas Cage – alternate broad popular movies with more offbeat fare, but they're less reliable as providers of entertainment, and their fans are fickle.

Pitt aficionados stay loyal because they trust his taste in movies. They know from reading interviews that he wants to be taken seriously, but they also sense that he never lost touch with the wide-eyed Missouri boy inside him – the tow-headed kid who sat on the hood of his parents' car at the drive-in, munching contraband popcorn and grinning up at the screen. They hope Pitt will stay in touch with that child indefinitely.   • 65

BOOK II

THE MOVIES

SEVEN

The plot sounds like the plot of a lot of movies: an impulsive young detective (Brad Pitt) and a wizened older mentor (Morgan Freeman) navigate a labyrinth of big city depravity to find a notorious serial killer. There was no reason for moviegoers to expect this big-budget horror epic to be anything but routine, yet the finished product made a number of year-end Ten Best lists and became an international phenomenon.

The tale begins, as all serial killer narratives do, with the discovery of the first victim – a grotesquely overweight man slumped over a kitchen table in his cramped slum home. It looks like an accidental death, or perhaps a suicide. But Detective Mills (Pitt, whose low-key machismo and slightly lunkheaded confidence are profoundly McQueenish) and Somerset (a typically superb Freeman in yet another Voice of Reason role) suspect it's murder most foul. And they're correct. On further investigation, they discover that the stiff was forced to eat himself to death; a second check of the dead man's house reveals a word scrawled on the wall behind the refrigerator: Gluttony. New victims are discovered at the rate of one per day, and each death is tied to one of the Bible's "Seven" deadly sins: Sloth, Greed, Pride, and so forth. Clearly, Mills and Somerset are dealing with a killer who has a demon's bloodlust, a monk's patience, and a performance artist's sense of style.

In the meantime, Somerset, who's a week away from retirement, and Mills, a hothead who recently moved to the city from a small town and fears not being taken seriously by his fellow detectives, get to know each other, moving through dislike and distrust into mutual respect. There's also a domestic subplot that turns out to be more important than it appears on first glance. Mills' beautiful and kindhearted young wife (Gwyneth Paltrow) dislikes the scale and pace of city life and feels both friendless and helpless. She takes an instant liking to Somerset and tells him a secret her husband hasn't heard: She's pregnant.

Her disclosure has thematic implications that Walker's murky, rather juvenile screenplay can't begin to address. The film posits the modern city as a moral cesspool that breeds agony, disappointment, sickness and death. It's a rigidly moralistic, even Puritan attitude, and "Seven" cheats quite a bit in articulating it; the city

Pitt's climactic scene in "Seven" proved his mettle as an actor. Within a matter of a few moments, he registers grief, fear and rage — then propels the film toward a downbeat ending so rarely seen in mainstream Hollywood that it knocks the breath out of you.

The film posits the modern city as a moral cesspool that

looks hellish, all right, but only because the filmmakers have photographed it through a scrim of gore and filth. A similar kind of cheating exists in the script's depiction of the killer, John Doe (Kevin Spacey), whose implacability and supercompetence make Hannibal Lecter look like a schlemiel. We are asked to believe, for instance, that Doe could visit the Sloth victim's apartment every day for a year without being identified; and that despite being "independently wealthy," he'd still check out books from the public library. Yet Spacey's stunning performance, which mixes arrogance and eerie calm in equal measure, enables us to suspend disbelief.

So does Pitt and Freeman's teamwork. Although both characters are types endemic to by-the-numbers cop films, the actors inhabit them completely and refuse to conform to our expectations. Freeman is tender-hearted and intellectual, but he's not a doddering oldster in need of coddling (like Danny Glover in the "Lethal Weapon" series). His mind is his weapon of choice, and he clearly loves unholstering it. His contemplative, confident, yet nonegocentric attitude suggests a number of great fictional detectives, specifically Sherlock Holmes. He seems equally at ease striding through muddy slums and sliding into a carrel

at the downtown library for a long night of research. And though he warms to Mills, one never senses that Somerset intends to become his bosom buddy. He maintains a cordial but distant professional air that's exactly right.

Pitt holds up his end of the relationship by resisting the impulse to make Mills yet another cop whose street smarts make up for his lack of education. On those rare occasions when he indulges his impulses, he tends to complicate matters rather than simplify them. And the final scene, which places Mills in a situation that demands an almost superhuman show of restraint, brilliantly articulates the difference between understanding the right response and actually carrying it out.

Best of all is the way "Seven" delineates the detectives' respective world views. Mills is a young cynic, strategically cynical because he's just been dropped into an urban hellhole after serving a stint in the boonies. We sense his hardboiled attitude is partly a pose designed to reassure himself that he's really as tough as he hopes. Somerset, who has logged three decades on the force and worked on hundreds of homicide cases, is entitled to a certain amount of pessimism,

The rapport between Pitt and Morgan Freeman wasn't all scripted. The two men developed a mutual respect and liking for one another during the film.

breeds agony, disappointment, sickness and death.

Pitt's and Freeman's characters come straight out of Cop/Buddy Films 101, but the actors refuse to play it by the book, giving us more than we expect.

but he rejects it. The fight isn't easy, though – especially once John Doe starts leaving bodies around like giant, gruesome calling cards; Freeman's magnificently expressive face registers the awful difficulty of maintaining hope while living in the belly of a world bound for hell.

Despite its missteps, oversimplifications, and rhetorical hyperbole, "Seven" is furiously convincing – and, more improbably, smart and classy, mainly due to its direction. Fincher concedes the repugnance of the killer's actions and the perversity of his damaged mind, but he also makes the disfigured corpses and their discovery sites oddly seductive, so that the viewer is at once disgusted and fascinated, and forced to actually think about the atrocities on display rather than merely recoil in simpleminded disgust. Fincher's world view is vastly more sophisticated and contradictory than Walker's script, which amounts to little more than a sermon on sin so trite, retrograde and transparently rigged that even an 18th century Puritan minister might deem it slanted. (The message of the film is: Stay the hell out of the city if you know what's good for you, kid.)

Fincher, Khondji and their technical support crew create an alternate universe of pure fright. From Howard Shore's the-world-is-coming-to-an-end score to the jumpy, artifact-strewn opening credits to the horrific finale – which ends the story on a downbeat note rarely seen outside the realm of adult comic books – every aspect of the film is geared towards unbalancing the viewer. It's an stylishly nasty creepshow that invades your rational mind like a virus.   • 71

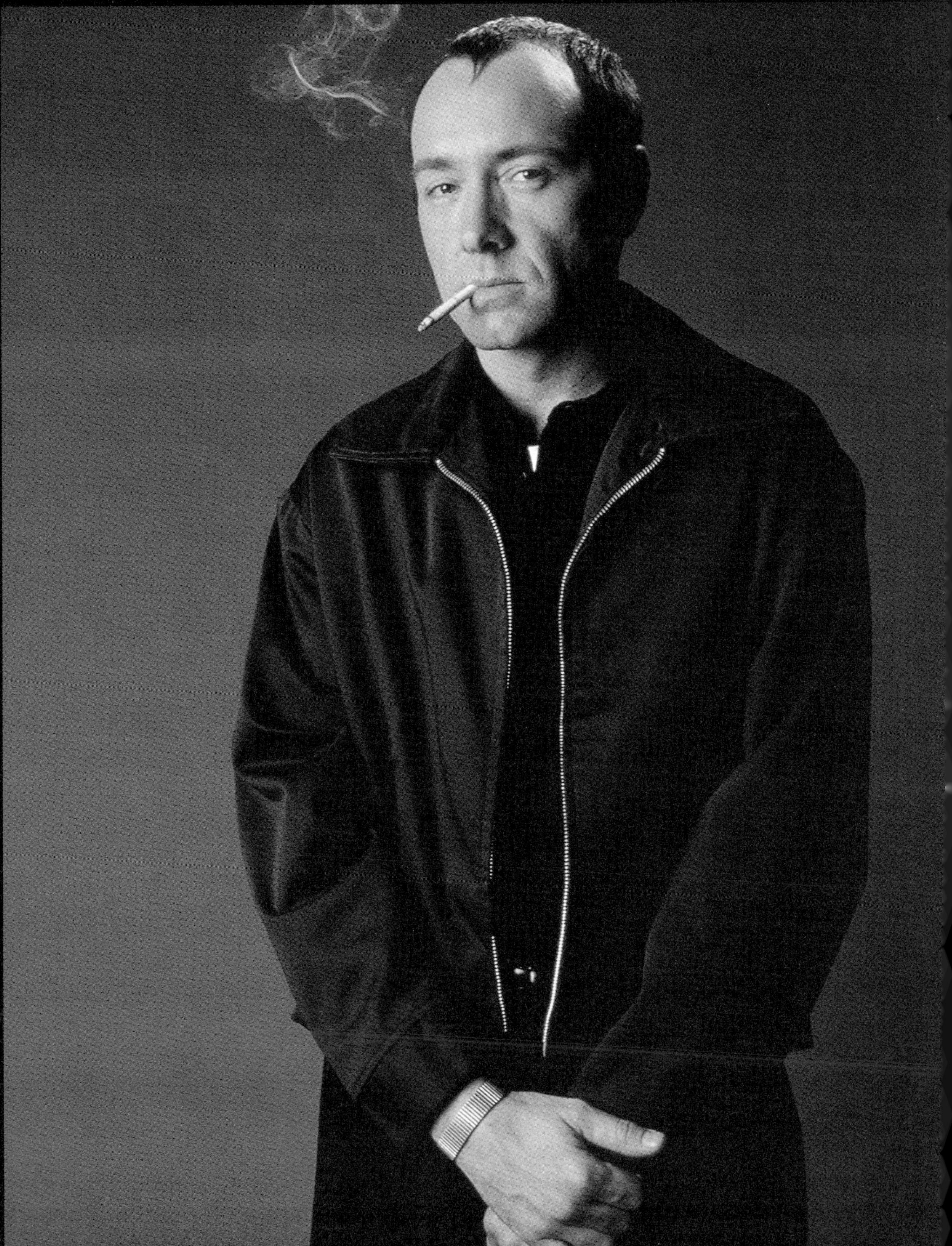

S P KEVIN A C E Y

b. South Orange, New Jersey, 1959. **"Seven"** (1995). One of the finest character actors in the cinema, Spacey built his career to a crescendo that finally reached the Academy Award pinnacle when he copped the Best Supporting Actor trophy for "The Usual Suspects." In the hands of a lesser talent, the film's secret easily would've leaked out too soon with one false gesture or misplaced glance.

TweLVe

A surprise hit for former Monty Python collaborator Terry Gilliam, this science fiction parable is drawn from a French short film by Chris Marker, who told his tale entirely with altered still photographs. It's about a time travelling ex-convict named James Cole (Bruce Willis), sent by his dictatorial masters several decades in the future to study the near demise of the human race in 1996, which supposedly occurred at the hands of a biological terrorist group called the Army of the Twelve Monkeys.

In this movie's version of temporal hopscotching, it is impossible to tinker with destiny; the best James can do is study the origins of the deadly virus, which spread across the world in a few short months and wiped out 99 percent of the population, then take the information back to the future so his bosses can work up a cure.

The time travel process is imprecise, though. James keeps landing in advance of 1996 and encountering people whose lives he will touch years later. They include a babbling doomsayer named Jeffrey Goines (Brad Pitt, with screwed-up eyes and Steve Buscemi's speed-freak diction), whom James meets while trapped in a mental institution; Jeffrey's dad (Christopher Plummer), a brilliant virologist whose laboratory might have been the source of the deadly virus; and Dr. Kathryn Railly (Madeleine Stowe), a criminal psychologist who first helps, then hinders, then joins James in his meandering quest. The actual time travelling isn't handled with much fuss; there are no computer-animated morphing sequences or bolts of cartoon lightning. Usually, James will just be standing somewhere one minute and be gone the next.

What makes "12 Monkeys" substantively different from other pictures on this theme – from "It's a Wonderful Life" to "Terminator 2" – is that each time James runs into the supporting characters, they've changed, sometimes because of meeting him and sometimes for their own reasons. There's also a very strong hint that nothing that happens to James is actually real – that he's merely a present-day lunatic locked inside his own demented fantasy world.

But with Gilliam at the helm, that world is stunningly detailed, distinctively personal, and hypnotic in its forcefulness. Whether a scene takes place in the future, the past, or the present, all his visual signatures are firmly in place – bulbous lenses that make people and places seem frighteningly huge, low-angle shots gazing up in awe at authority, the god's-eye views of our heroes being prepped for incaceration or torture. Willis even gets strapped in an elevated electric chair at one point, just like poor Sam Lowry in "Brazil."

The script does manage to be faithful to its source, however, making only minor changes to please contemporary audiences (fear of nuclear war is replaced by fear of plague; the finale is open-ended rather than stylishly pessimistic).

While one could see a familial resemblance in many of Pitt's roles, Jeffrey Goines strolls into his canon of characters like an uninvited ex-brother-in-law crashing the family reunion.

MonKeYs

75

It feels like the work of a stargazing old man, hardened by

Husband-wife screenwriting team Janet and David Peoples are refreshingly committed to the idea that a Hollywood-produced genre film needn't necessarily coddle its viewers. (David Peoples has a sterling track record in this area; he penned "Blade Runner" and was nominated for an Oscar for writing Clint Eastwood's western masterwork "Unforgiven.")

The narrative works on several levels: as a satiric sendup of revolutionary politics and end-of-the-millenium angst; as an action-packed adventure epic; as an offbeat romance about a lonely man and a lonely woman coming together against all odds; and as a meditation on reincarnation, guilt and destiny. But it never relinquishes its core of tenderness – its sympathy for small people caught up in unfathomably gigantic events.

For the first time in his career, Gilliam doesn't let his own stylistic curlicues over-whelm the movie. The film has a funhouse-mirror chaotic quality early on, when both James and the audience are adjusting to the terrors of time travel and the revelations of history. But as the movie progresses, Gilliam stops tilting, swinging and whirling his camera, and the cuts become less frenzied. The film accustoms us to living in a world gone mad, even encourages us to embrace it and appreciate it. There's a ghostly beauty in the apocalyptic sequences early on, when James explores a depopulated Philadelphia overrun with escaped zoo animals, yet there's a different kind of beauty when his camera prowls the hallways of the asylum, the opulent interiors of Jeffrey Goines' country estate, and the garbage-strewn streets of contemporary American flophouses and ghetto streets. James and Kathryn get threatened with imprisonment, rape, assault, murder and other terrors, yet Gilliam never rubs our nose in their terror. Like a great 19th-century novelist, he takes a broad view and sees the society – perhaps the species – and not simply the plight of individuals. There's more compassion for humanity in this film than in any work

experience but not yet closed off from good humor.

he's done before. It feels like the work of a stargazing old man, hardened by experience but not yet closed off from good humor, sentiment and empathy.

Gilliam says he loves people, but he gave critics little reason to believe it until now; his George Grosz thirst for caricature, honed over a decade of animating for Monty Python, was so overpowering that he always came off as a bit of a misanthrope. ("Brazil," as brilliant as it was, sometimes seemed

Unlike his earlier films, director Terry Gilliam doesn't allow his stylistic vision to overwhelm the actors in the film.

more interested in the fascist masters than the hapless citizens, perhaps because the places where the fascists hung out looked better on camera.) But "Twelve Monkeys" is the most tender-hearted film he's ever made. James, Kathryn, Jeffrey and company encounter dozens and dozens of bizarre characters during their travels, some rich, some poor, some black, some white, some helpful, some malevolent. Gilliam may puff them all up into archetypes, but he doesn't condescend to them or use them to score cheap, cruel jokes. On some level, he loves them all; he shows affection even towards his

villains (which include Frank Gorshin as an insane asylum administrator and Paul Meshejian as a condescending police detective), perhaps because he realizes that in the screenplay's grand scheme, knaves and idiots are as helpless as heroes; no matter what humans do, destiny proceeds dispassionately with its plans.

That view sounds fatalistic, but accepting it doesn't mean condemning yourself to a life of despair. The solution is to live life moment to moment and savor each one, large or small. "Twelve Monkeys" has more small moments than any Gilliam movie – moments when characters simply gaze at each other and smile, or touch each other, or revel in their surroundings. There's an astonishing sequence midway through when Kathryn and James drive along a highway at night, talking about their predicament and listening to songs on the radio, including "I Found my Thrill (On Blueberry Hill)" and "It's a Wonderful World." As James hears what he calls "the music of the 20th century," he begins to cry. It's Willis' finest moment as an actor – understated, unaffected, and improbably touching – but it's only one fine moment in a movie full of them; it's one fine moment in a movie that finds greatness in small matters and calm faith in momentous events.   • 77

b. Minneapolis, Minnesota, 1940.
"Twelve Monkeys" (1995). Although his most famous film prior to "Twelve Monkeys" was the Orwellian "Brazil," his brilliant vision deserved the more apt moniker "Orson Wellesian." Unfortunately, he is only just now developing a sense of narrative. Once he allows his actors and storyline to hold their own, Gilliam may be capable of ultimately creating the "Citizen Kane" of our time.

TERRY GILLIAM

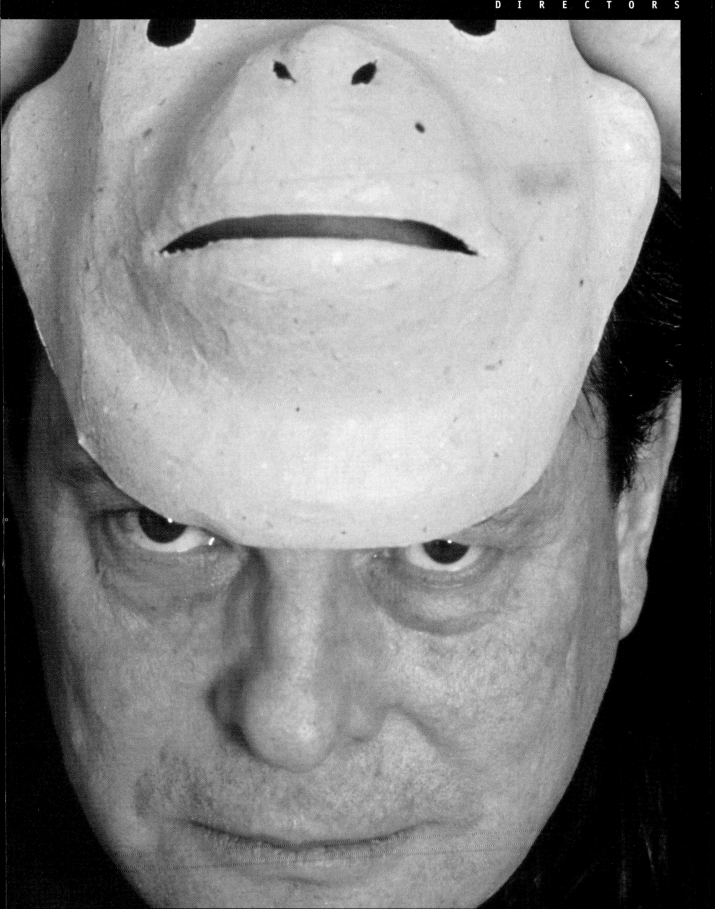

Madeleine STOWE

b. Eagle Rock, California, 1959. **"Twelve Monkeys"** (1995). Her brave, romantic, bold character in "The Last of the Mohicans" lifted her out of the "just another pretty face" rank of actresses.

LEG

Set in rural Montana before and after World War I, "Legends of the Fall" would make an intriguing double-bill with "A River Runs Through It," and not just because of its setting; its nostalgic recreation of a bygone time and place jockeys for prominence with an unabashedly syrupy emotionalism, plot contrivances aplenty, and a brand of hero worship that mixes Nitzschean awe and the tragic romanticism of Emily Bronte. The end result suggests MacLean's novella rewritten by Ayn Rand.

The epic narrative centers on the rising and falling fortunes of the Ludlow family. The clan's patriarch, William Ludlow (Anthony Hopkins), has recently retired from a

Pitt seized the moment with "Legends of the Fall," using its syrupy melodramatics to full effect in creating a star vehicle for himself.

ENDS OF THE FALL

career in the cavalry, during which he witnessed many atrocities against Indians. The experience caused him to loathe the United States government and anyone who would place the power of written law in the hands of self-interested and cruel individuals.

Ludlow has three sons. The eldest, Alfred (Aidan Quinn), is quiet, reflective, and confident, and seems bound for a career as a leader. The youngest Ludlow, Samuel (Henry Thomas), is a bright-eyed lad who hopes, like Norman MacLean in "A River Runs Through It," to distinguish himself as a scholar. The middle child, Tristan (Brad Pitt), is a wild, rugged, muscular loner, at one with nature and the universe but driven, like Paul MacLean, by invisible demons. Since childhood, he has nurtured a running grudge against a great grizzly bear that he tried to kill when he was only eight years old. The movie's narrator,

an Indian named One-Stab (Gordon Tootoosis) who lives and works on the Ludlow property, sees this as evidence that Tristan has "a wildness in him," and nothing Tristan says or does during the rest of his life contradicts this observation. Like the James Dean characters in "East of Eden" and "Giant," Tristan is a one-man vessel into which all of the novelist and directors' cockamamie ideas about mankind's primitive impulses can be poured.

Occasional squabbles aside, the Ludlows get along with each other fairly well until the arrival of Susannah (Julia Ormond), a raven-haired Brit engaged to marry Samuel. Shortly after, the three brothers – all of whom fancy themselves the ideal man for Susannah – go off to war, and in a wholly improbable battle sequence (which requires Alfred, Tristan and Samuel all to be present in the same small area of France) the youngest Ludlow is killed.

Tristan, who was charged by his father with protecting Samuel, goes berserk, scalping Germans and taking his own brother's heart home in a box for burial; though the sequence is inherently silly, director Ed Zwick suffuses it in mysticism and meaning, pushing for powerhouse emotion and implying, as he will throughout the film, that Tristan somehow has a deeper, finer and more savage appreciation of life than the other members of his family.

Back home, the Ludlows split apart, with Alfred striking out on his own to pursue business and political ambitions and Tristan staying near the family property, guarding his own privacy zealously but succumbing to Susannah's charms. He responds to her love for him by leaving Montana to travel around the world; his journey is depicted as a kind of extended primal scream travelogue: When Tristan isn't lashed to a ship's

83

mast during a violent sea storm howling at the heavens, he's curled up in a tiny bed with two brown-skinned women or trading peace pipe hits with wizened tribesmen on a New Guinea beach. He comes home to find that his father has suffered a stroke (a change Hopkins conveys by scrunching up his face and talking like Popeye) and Susannah has married Alfred. She's desperately unhappy and still pines for Tristan. Alfred has become a representative of the same mindless government authoritarianism his father despises; he has become a senator by jumping on the Prohibition bandwagon, and this puts him in direct opposition to Tristan, who is supporting his family (he's married to the daughter of one of his father's ranch hands and has children) by bootlegging whiskey. In a

steadily escalating series of confrontations, Tristan and two of his father's employees kill several local policemen; Tristan's wife and child are killed for revenge; and Tristan kills the men who killed his family. The film ends with a confrontation on the Ludlow family homestead, with pop Ludlow blowing a "revenooer" right out of his boots and Alfred appearing out of nowhere, like Van Helflin at the finale of "Shane," to kill the last remaining government agent. One Stab's narration informs us that in time, everyone close to Tristan died, and that their love for the elusive hunk was at least partly to blame. "He was the rock they broke themselves against," One Stab says. Tristan gets the movie's final freeze-frame; as a senior citizen wandering the Alaskan wilderness, he comes across a big grizzly, whips out

his knife and goes mano-a-bearo and loses.

What can possibly be said in defense of such silliness? Nothing, and the fact that Ed Zwick doesn't even try helps explain the allure of "Legends of the Fall." Nothing in the movie is treated with anything remotely approaching irony. We are meant to take everything that happens at face value – to laugh when the film tells us to laugh, grieve when it tells us to grieve, and swoon when it tells us to swoon. Like "East of Eden" and "Giant," the tone is sober and reflective, but the events themselves are overblown to the point of parody. It's interesting to compare Zwick's film with its source, the novella by Jim Harrison. A mystical tough-guy writer of the Ernest Hemingway-Norman Mailer school, the writer conveys every detail of the screenplay and many more in less than 90 pages. Events that require several scenes in the movie are dispensed with in a single paragraph by Harrison – sometimes a few lines. The compactness of the writing

Pitt certainly learned the importance of making an entrance in the film. His first meeting with Susannah (Julia Ormond) was just one of three.

sober and reflective, but the events themselves are overblown.

Pitt's overpowering screen presence relegated the traditional "sex object" role filled by Julia Ormond virtually neuter.

(and its relentlessly deadpan style) are strategic: by narrating the Ludlow family history with rigorous austerity and emotional restraint, the author lends patently absurd occurrences a veneer of class and wisdom. (Compared to Harrison's writing, the Old Testament seems warm and cuddly.) Though many key events have been altered for the film version, the book has been transferred more or less faithfully, except for Zwick's tone, which is moony and awestruck, particularly in its treatment of Tristan.

Intriguingly, though, the movie doesn't seem so much a reworking of its source as a less pretentious, more truthful rendering of it; the film "Legends of the Fall" is absurd and knows it, where the book was absurd and pretended not to know it. The facade of stony omniscience crumbles to reveal an unusually macho romance novel, complete with unlikely chance meetings and all-too-convenient, last-minute changes of heart. The cast gets into the spirit of things – particularly Ormond, who gives a trembling, weepy performance reminiscent of Merle Oberon in "Wuthering Heights," and Pitt, who invests a highly unlikely character with a certain rugged credibility. Only Anthony Hopkins embarrasses himself, playing Colonel Ludlow with too much crusty authority early on and too much shriveled pugnaciousness post-stroke; as in "Bram Stroker's Dracula," he turns in a performance that's not a contribution to the film's mood, but an unknowing caricature of it.   •   85

ANTHONY HOPKINS

b. Port Talbot, Wales 1937. **"Legends of the Fall"** (1994). Is he a present-tense Lord Olivier, or simply an upper class version of Michael Caine? For the most part (or parts), Hopkins appears the former, whether speaking of his Oscar-winning Hannibal Lecter, his even creepier psycho in "Magic," or his handful of recent period pieces such as "Remains of the Day." Too often, though, he seems to fall into the Caine trap of accepting just about any part that comes with a paycheck.

b. Epsom, Surrey, U.K., 1965. **"Legends of the Fall"** (1994). Almost as soon as the beautiful English lass with the sparkling smile arrived in Los Angeles, studios began casting her in a series of love-interest roles in "Legends of the Fall," "Sabrina" and "First Knight." Although unquestionably beautiful, she has yet to turn in a performance capable of capturing the imagination.

julia
ormond

Interview with the Vampire

Based on the best-selling 1976 novel by Anne Rice, this supernatural epic was a hot property in Hollywood for more than 15 years until record and movie mogul David Geffen packaged it for Irish director Neil Jordan ("The Crying Game") and toothy superstar Tom Cruise. The latter was at the peak of his influence following the phenomenal success of the John Grisham movie "The Firm," and thought playing the coveted role of Rice's all-powerful, bloodsucking playboy Lestat would prove he really was as versatile as his fans liked to claim.

Like Rice's novel, the film is cast as an extended flashback told by Louis (Brad Pitt), a French-American ne'er do well who was bitten two centuries ago by a powerful bloodsucker named Lestat (Tom Cruise) while roaming New Orleans' French quarter. Louis quickly goes through Elisabeth Kubler-Ross' five stages of death – denial, anger, depression, bargaining, acceptance – and discovers that vampires are not the solitary creatures portrayed in mythology, but members of an extended international underground community with time-honored rules of conduct. Lestat enjoys Louis' company, although he isn't especially nice to him; he treats him as an acolyte and a stooge, alternately lecturing him on the ways of the undead and ridiculing his squeamish attitude towards all things vampirish.

Like Satan in the Rolling Stones' "Sympathy for the Devil," Lestat has been around for long, long years and has seen many a man seal his fate. But poor Louis never wanted to be a vampire and struggles incessantly to come to grips with his destiny. It isn't easy because Lestat keeps acting the part of Eddie Haskell to Louis' Wally Cleaver. Every time the poor hero thinks he's reached a state of moral truce with his condition, Lestat enters bearing new innocent blood and forces him to make yet another moral compromise. The elder vampire has made it his mission to chip away at whatever dregs of moral resolve Louis has left, and he eventually succeeds. Jordan's script nicely empha-sizes a point that Rice's dynamic, flowery language obscured in the book: when all is said and done, Lestat and Louis are essentially comic figures, and borderline incompetent at that – simultaneously brutal and dimwitted, like the Ray Liotta and Joe Pesci characters in "Goodfellas." They're constantly squabbling at the least opportune times; Lestat is always killing people on impulse, leaving the vampires no choice but to burn whole buildings down to cover their tracks.

Louis' tolerance reaches its limits when Lestat makes a vampire of a nine-year old girl named Claudia (Kirsten Dunst). This drives home a point Louis had been ponder-ing all along: that immortality comes at the cost of maturity, growth and honestly earned experience. Rather than immortality, undead status offers a kind of endless time-out; the joy of living a life

While "Interview with the Vampire" was Pitt's highest grossing film to date, his performance as the undead Louis also was his most lifeless.

beyond the reach of polite society is overshadowed by the burden of knowing that other, more meaningful aspects of being human – love, family life, the acquisition of wisdom – are forever beyond reach. The most heartbreaking illustration of this notion comes when the vampires wander through a red light district of New Orleans. Claudia spies a prostitute and marvels at her adult body and asks if she will ever look like that. The answer, tragically, is no, and Louis is wracked with guilt and shame over having to provide it. He takes Claudia under his wing, and together, the three vampires form a perverse facsimile of a nuclear family, with Claudia as the wide-eyed child; Louis as a put-upon male mommy; and Lestat as a classic bad dad who is absent much of the time and causes chaos and misery whenever he's present.

The plot flips over when Claudia kills Lestat in a fit of resentful rage, leaving both Louis and the girl, for all practical purposes, fatherless. They find their way to Paris and fall in with a vampire theater troupe whose denizens include two Lestat-like power mongers (ably played by longtime Jordan stock company member Stephen Rea and Spanish heartthrob Antonio Banderas, whose icy charisma and seductively purring voice may make the viewer wonder why he didn't play Lestat). The troupe performs feats of "magic" – actually a grim, supernatural variant of showing-off – for select crowds of thrill-seekers. They ultimately prove even less interested in pondering moral questions than the late, not-so-lamented Lestat.

Louis gets caught in a power struggle with the group, and as punishment, he is walled into a crypt to spend the rest of eternity in excruciating torment. Claudia and her mother are locked in a storage space with a window. In a fit of rage, Louis breaks free and torches the place. Then he makes like a Missouri wheat farmer at harvest time and eviscerates the few escaping vampires with a gigantic scythe. Returning home to New Orleans, he finds Lestat still alive, but wasting away – a shadow of his former self. The interview ends on an open-ended note, with more than a hint of sequel possibilities.

"Interview with the Vampire" is a less dynamic story than the book – more a collection of images and feelings. Jordan eschews a dynamic plot in favor of a series of setpieces and atmospheric montages; he's more interested in recreating the look and sound of an undead universe than in

Christian Slater stepped into the role of the interviewer after River Phoenix took an overdose of heroin and died on the sidewalk outside an L.A. club.

nd resourceful actor stuck in a passive role.

At first glance, Pitt seems merely miscast as the doleful Louis, the reluctant vampire. In the final analysis, though, the role would've sucked the blood from just about anyone.

thrilling the audience or teaching ironic moral lessons. There are a few moments that are repugnant and spectacular – two vampires clinging to each other as the rising sun turns them to dust; Lestat's killing at the hands of Claudia and Louis, which unleashes a torrent of velvet blood. Despite Jordan's obvious fascination with and sympathy for society's outsiders – a trait showcased to better effect in his taboo-busting trilogy, "Mona Lisa," "The Miracle" and "The Crying Game" – we rarely feel a primal emotional connection to Rice's undead nomads.

The blame isn't Jordan's, necessarily; he directs with considerable passion and wit and has an obvious understanding of the source material. But the leads, who either are poorly cast or badly directed, fail to support him. Actors are the intermediaries between the filmmaker and the audience; they grant abstract ideas flesh-and-blood form and pull a film together. Yet Cruise and Pitt remain one-note and rather aloof throughout, and as a result, some of Jordan's more interesting ideas just swirl through the movie pointlessly,

palpable but undefined, like the haze that hangs over the streets of New Orleans. One can't help but feel a certain sympathy for Pitt, a game and resourceful actor stuck in a passive role; but it's also difficult to imagine a more energetic, even hammy actor – a Kenneth Branagh, for instance, or Jason Patric – investing the material with energy and flair.

The failings of Cruise's performance are more clear-cut: He has chosen to play up Lestat's bitchy humor at the expense of his magnetism, which robs the role of the mysterious, deadly qualities it should have had. Cruise is a workmanlike actor who can do

wonders in the right part, but though he has many useful qualities, raw sensuality is not among them. Lestat is a strutting bad boy who gets off on his own nastiness but is also charming and forceful enough to convince other people to overlook it; he's the James Dean of the undead. Cruise suggests a student council president in Halloween drag, and over time, his shrill voice and nerdy giggle grows almost as tiresome as Pitt's flat, midwestern narration.

One emerges from "Interview with the Vampire" shaken but not stirred. It's a visually sumptuous horror show that has plenty of blood but not enough heart.   •   **93**

AntonioBanderas

b. Malaga, Spain, 1960. **"Interview with the Vampire"** (1994). Antonio Banderas appeared in 15 films and was a major star in his native Spain before catching the eye of American casting directors in director Pedro Almodovar's "Women on the Verge of a Nervous Breakdown" in 1988. By 1994 he had polished his English and made a bid for U.S. stardom in "The Mambo Kings."

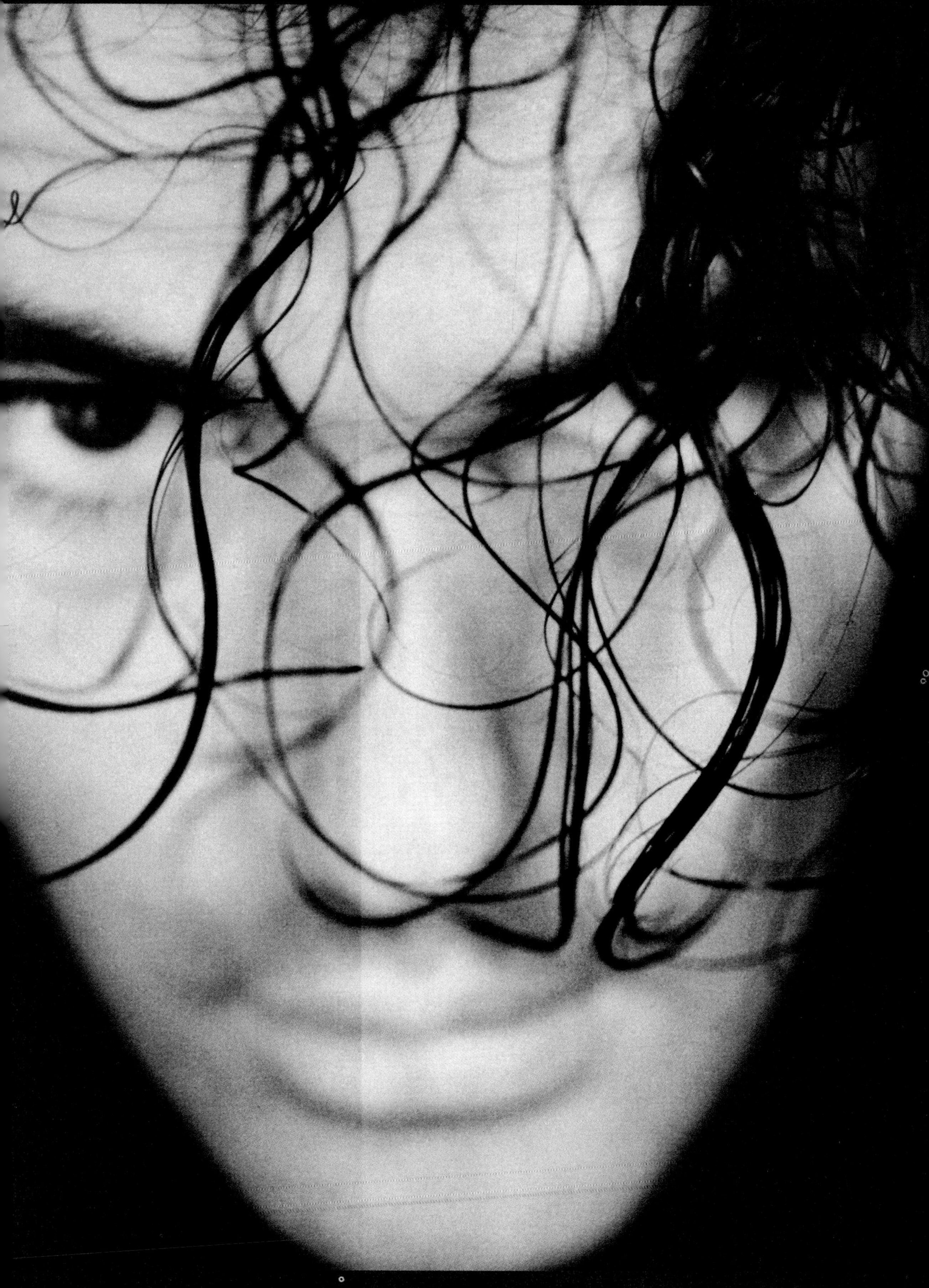

b. New York, New York, 1969. **"Interview with the Vampire"** (1994). **"True Romance"** (1993). He survived his teen-heartthrob phase intact, only to spend the four years between 1989's "Heathers" through "True Romance" intent on perfecting his Jack Nicholson impression. "Vampire" seemed to shake him out of that spell, as well as his wisely chosen follow-up "Murder in the First" opposite Kevin Bacon.

C H R I S T I A N

S L A T E R

Kalif

ornia

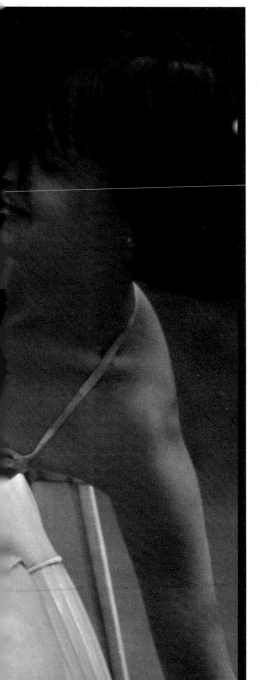

A long with his cameo as a goggle-eyed stoner in "True Romance" that same year, this movie demonstrated that Pitt could do more than strut around shirtless and pout soulfully. Directed by Dominic Sena from a script by Tim Metcalfe (who wrote "Revenge of the Nerds"), "Kalifornia" is a glitzy parable about American violence and liberal guilt, built around a too-easy irony: A man fascinated by killers becomes friends with a real killer, then must embrace his own repressed, violent impulses.

Brian Kessler (David Duchovny) is an academic fascinated by mass murderers; his girlfriend Carrie Laughlin (Michelle Forbes) is a Robert Mapplethorpeish photographer. They decided to finance a road trip to California by visiting famous mass murder sites, documenting them in writing and photographs, and turning the results into a book. They post a notice asking for another

Juliette Lewis outshone Pitt badly in "Too Young to Die," their first film together. By "Kalifornia," he was more than a match for her.

couple to join them to share expenses. Unfortunately, the first person to see the notice is Early Grayce (Pitt), a brutish redneck ex-con who lives in a trailer park with his slow-witted girlfriend, Adele Corners (Juliette Lewis). They need to flee town fast because Early is planning to kill his nagging landlord. So the low-rent lovers join the highbrow scholars in the official vehicle of road trip movies, the oversized American convertible, and make like Jack Kerouac.

It's not hard to guess what will happen next. The travelers forge tentative bonds despite their differences. Liberated Carrie gives Adele a stylish haircut and hears of her love for Early, who beats her only when she "deserves it. Brian becomes strangely fond of Early, whose rough masculinity he finds bookishly fascinating.

But Early can't keep his violent impulses in check. He murders a man in a filling station restroom to get money to pay for gas, savagely beats a bully who taunts Brian in a bar, and barrages Carrie with sexually insinuating comments and glances throughout the story. It's only a matter of time until the academics figure out what kind of monster they're carting along the interstates, and it all leads to a predictably savage showdown at an abandoned nuclear test range, with Brian and Early going at it like Godzilla and Megalon until the bookworm finally pumps the killer full of lead.

"Kalifornia" is a movie full of shallow symbolism: cheap cross-cutting between Carrie and Brian examining murder sites and Early acting violently or strange; turbocharged widescreen images of desolate landscapes that resemble photos from a brochure advertising the Ridley Scott Directing School; and the showdown at the nuclear test site, which tries to forge a link between Early Grayce's sadism and America's violent past but fails miserably. The film is both hip and square, self-conscious and clueless; every scene and character fits into a preconceived narrative slot, and twists occur with clockwork predictability, leading to the inevitable "Cape Fear"-style finale.

The movie isn't so much directed as art directed; in "Kalifornia" — unlike "Seven," which also was obsessed with its own look, feel and sound — the stylistic tics don't grow organically from the storyline. Instead, they're grafted onto the plot for no other reason than to satisfy the filmmakers' urge for striking visuals. The beginning, which shows Early dropping a cement block off a

Pitt's complex reading of Early Grayce blows away the screenplay's formulaic take on the character.

:reepy facial tics, off-kilter line readings, and feral stares.

David Duchovny filled the stock roll of "liberal pushed over the edge" with the dry humor that presaged his future stardom on "The X-Files."

highway bridge onto an unsuspecting motorist during a rainstorm, points up everything wrongheaded about Sena and Metcalfe's vision; they seem more interested in the texture of rain coursing through gutters, across roads and down over Early's face than in the murderous event or its consequences.

Ditto the scene when Early beats and stabs a man in a gas station restroom, which is lit and composed like an ad for Levi's 501 jeans. Strip away

Brian Kessler's prattling about humankind's dark side and you're left with a smugly hip arthouse variation on "Death Wish" and its imitators — films that pretend to investigate the nature of violence while reveling in it like hogs at a feed trough and that introduce a sensitive liberal character in the first scene only to place a gun in his hand in the last.

That said, the film does serve as a showcase for four fine actors. Duchovny's dry humor — exploited nicely in the long-running paranoid sci-fi series "The X-Files" — gives his nerdy character a welcome dash of human warmth. Forbes' husky voice and disbelieving stare

makes Carrie the most recognizably real character in the picture — an audience surrogate who sees through the nonsense on screen and struggles valiantly to leave it behind. Lewis inhabits the chirpy, clueless, terminally idiotic Adele so completely that audiences may be tempted to cheer her death. And Pitt's work is implosively self-contained — a bundle of creepy facial tics, off-kilter line readings, and feral stares that exist less to communicate with other people than to keep Early amused. In quieter moments, Pitt's performance suggests Early is more complicated, and more human, than the schematic script will admit. •   **101**

David
Duchovny

b. New York, New York, 1960. **"Kalifornia"** (1993). Dedicated watchers of strange television should've seen Duchovny's potential as a major cult star at least three years before he reached that status with his debut in 1993 as Fox Mulder on "The X-Files." In 1990, he dropped into the middle of the year-long "Twin Peaks" wierdness telethon as transvestite DEA agent Dennis/Denise Bryson.

A River *Runs Through* It

"Based on Norman MacLean's autobiographical novella, this film from Robert Redford tells the story of two brothers growing up in the wilds of Montana during the period before World War I. Craig Sheffer plays the narrator, Norman, a book-smart fellow who wants to leave his small town and become a teacher with cosmopolitan graces. Brad Pitt plays his younger brother, Paul, a free spirit. They both were taught by their minister father (Tom Skerritt) that fly-fishing is a metaphor for finding a state of grace. Paul finds it early on, though as an adult, the life he lives away from the river is chaotic, full of provo-

Director Robert Redford filmed Pitt with such haloed, backlit grace that some commentators drew the conclusion that Redford saw a little of himself in the younger man.

cations and occasional violence. Norman's life is more rational and sensible, but he fears he's not living it to its fullest and that he'll never attain the state of radiant peace his brother projects so effortlessly.

Of course, Paul isn't as placid as he appears, and the last hour of the film is dedicated to chronicling a steadily escalating series of misfortunes and miscalculations that will end in his inevitable death. Although Norman is positioned as the main character (and audience surrogate) and carries the burden of the movie's narration, it's Paul's film; every character in the movie is defined primarily through their feelings towards Paul, their attitude towards his self-destructive tendencies, and their willingness to worry about what happens to him.

For all the attention showered on him, Paul remains a tantalizing question mark — a golden-haired angel fallen to Earth, casting his fishing line into sparkling waters with a rhythm attuned to the invisible movements of God and nature. He is described by his brother as having found "grace" without any great expenditure of effort. Yet this accomplishment cannot protect him against his own irresponsible nature, nor can it assist others who want to save him. After a brief life spent running in place, Paul dies in a bar fight; the tragic event happens offscreen, which artfully obscures its meaning (and jibes with Redford's tendency to underplay plot points other directors might milk for cheap sentiment).

The film is a curious combination of wisdom and schmaltz. While Redford's clear-eyed approach is meant to pull the film together in the way that MacLean's authorial voice pulled the book together, it actually serves to underline the material's weaknesses of both

105

structure and vision. Like the book, the film is less a unified narrative than a collection of vignettes, most of which, fortunately, are involving and occasionally very funny.

What comes through most strongly is a legitimate sense of time and place. A prominent environmentalist, Redford obviously pines for America's rural past — a time before long-distance telephone connections and cheap transcontinental air travel, a time before automobiles and suburbs carved up the countryside into characterless clumps of plasticized living space. It was a time when one didn't have to make a special effort to appreciate the deep-rooted rituals of life — holidays, church, family get-togethers, births, marriages, deaths. They were woven into the fabric of everyday living— a notion woven directly into the film's voice-over narration, which stresses the importance of everyday pleasures and community concerns rather than long-range individualistic goals.

Norman's decision to head to Chicago to seek an education isn't portrayed dismissively, but as a momentous and possibly disruptive event in the MacLean family's existence; as Redford has noted, the MacLean brothers grew up during a time of seemingly limitless possibility, when an understanding of the Western canon conferred elder status on the scholar who achieved it, and the century's most profound breakthroughs in science had yet to extend their influence around the globe.

In a sense, Norman and Paul can be seen as representatives of different centuries. While

Pitt's understated acting complements Redford's understated direction. Even Paul's death, the film's climactic moment, occurs off-screen.

intact — one more mystery nobody will ever solve.

As Paul MacLean, Pitt represents our rural past. Craig Sheffer as Norman provides the 20th century foil — mobile, ambitious, and ultimately unfulfilled.

Norman is comfortable with change and aspires to be a sophisticated man of letters and perhaps even a world traveler, Paul is inextricably tied to the past — his own, his family's, and his town's. He seems happy where he is, writing columns for the local weekly and plying his luck down by the river. Told that he should go to Chicago to seek his fortune as a journalist (a place where, the narration wistfully informs us, there are "twelve daily newspapers"), he rejects it.

MacLean believed that grace could be achieved by cultivating an understanding and appreciation of life.

He doesn't squeeze his story for cheap melodrama; he prefers a distanced, nuanced, slightly aloof tone the good Reverend himself would have appreciated.

The leads all contribute solid work, though one is always conscious that Norman is too much the spectator, watching from afar as his more glamorous, soulful, tragic brother heads off towards his destiny.

The two leads struggle admirably with very different burdens. Craig Sheffer is entrusted with the role of witness and audience surrogate, which limits his chances for heroic action, but he carries himself with a very winning, weather-beaten charm and maturity that's rare in American movies. When we look at him, we can see the man he probably will become — a man much like his father, but with a more melancholy air. We sense that his talk about adventure and possibility is at least partly faked; his courtship with a local flapper named Jessie (Emily Lloyd) is full of moments when he seems appalled or frightened by her risky behavior. She seems more in tune with Paul, and if "A River Runs Through It" weren't based on a true story,

viewers could reasonably expect the two of them to become attracted to each other.

The role of Paul is equally vexing, and Pitt doesn't quite pull it off, not for lack of resourcefulness, but because the script doesn't always give him enough material to work with. The allure of his character stems from his inscrutability; though he's an easygoing sort, he politely deflects his brother's attempts to get inside his head and figure out what makes him tick. The character vanishes from the earth with all his enigmatic contradictions intact. He is one more mystery nobody will ever solve.

"A River Runs Through It" is a noble, thoughtful film, but ultimately as limited, emotionally, as the characters themselves.

Craig Sheffer

b. 1960. **"A River Runs Through It"** (1992). Unfortunately, Sheffer appears to be one of those actors whose breakthrough role also may end up being the only role for which he's remembered. As the narrator in "A River Runs Through It," he shares the spotlight with Pitt. Sheffer's played roles in nine feature films, a TV movie and a miniseries in the five years since, but you'd be hard-pressed to bring a single one to mind without at least a few hints.

THELMA & LOUISE

The story starts out like a lighthearted buddy movie. In Arkansas, two best friends – mild-mannered housewife Thelma (Geena Davis) and tough single waitress Louise (Susan Sarandon) – decide to take a short vacation together. At a roadside nightclub, Thelma gets drunk and dances with a swaggering cowboy named Harlan (Timothy Carhart) who later tries to rape her in the parking lot. Louise intervenes and shoots the man dead.

Louise convinces Thelma that the police will never believe their version of what happened. They rendezvous with Louise's boyfriend Jimmy, who gives the women a much-needed bundle of cash; but it's stolen hours later by a handsome hitchhiker named J.D. (Brad Pitt), who spent the night with Louise in the women's hotel room. Out of options, they turn to armed robbery, pursued every step of the way by the FBI, assorted local cops, and an Arkansas trooper (Harvey Keitel). What began as a vacation turns into a Butch-and-Sundance style crime spree; a declaration of independence from male-dominated society; and a spectacular suicide pact whose meanings will be debated for generations to come.

The film became a locus of controversy, sparking countless op-ed pieces, a cover story in *Time*, and heaven knows how many spats between men and women across America. Written by Callie Khouri (a first-timer who won an Oscar for her efforts) and directed by master visual stylist Ridley Scott ("Alien" and "Blade Runner"), "Thelma and Louise" dealt in broad feminist themes that struck a very raw nerve. And like "Bonnie and Clyde," a smash-hit road movie it closely resembles, "Thelma and Louise" unapologetically served up its protagonists as pop culture antiheroines who said and did things other women had dreamed about for

Pitt didn't even rack up 15 minutes of screen time in "Thelma and Louise," but he capitalized on every second with an unforgettable characterization in a pivotal role.

110

generations.

Besides the central plotline, Scott, Khouri and company indulge in many amusing side jokes that stick it to the pigs of the world. When Thelma calls Darryl from the road, he acts furious with her, but he's apparently not angry enough to quit watching a college football game on TV. The women humiliate a swaggering cop with mirrored sunglasses who pulls them over in Arizona and tries to intimidate them through sheer force of machismo; they pull a gun on him and make him climb into the trunk of his own police car. Before they lock the trunk, Thelma asks the cop if he has a wife. He says he does. "Well, you be nice to her," Thelma says cheerfully. "My husband wasn't nice to me, and look how I turned out!" The most

blatant crowd-pleasing moment comes near the end, when Thelma and Louise once again encounter a lascivious truck driver who's been ogling them on the road for days. They flirtatiously invite him to pull over, then pull their tiny handguns and fire on his truck; to their surprise as well as his, the bullets hit the vehicle's gas tank and destroy it in a gigantic cloud of orange flame.

These scenes gave ammunition to detractors who complained that "Thelma and Louise" was a glossy sham, a vulgar rebellion fantasy masquerading as a serious sociological statement. Its heroines, critics charged, reveled in the same violent impulses they claimed to loathe in men.

The movie's male characters, except for Harvey Keitel's sympathetic police detective, were portrayed as either buffoons, hunks or pigs, which meant "Thelma and Louise" was morally no better than the films it was supposed to stand in contrast to – macho action pictures where the only women in sight are girlfriends, hookers and corpses. A *New York Times* article even claimed the film's sentimentally tragic finale wasn't as inevitable as the filmmakers liked to think; in real life, the women probably would have gotten off with a light jail sentence, even probation.

All these gripes seem silly in retrospect. With its densely detailed, widescreen vistas, bubbly pop soundtrack, and rain that seems to start and stop to suit the characters' moods, "Thelma and Louise" never pretends to be a realistic movie. It is defiantly larger than life – an alternately brutal, satiric, and tender fable about how men and women look at, and treat, one another. And its cast straddles the line between intimate observation and cartoonish posturing with great skill. Sarandon and Davis' teamwork won them both

Although the screenplay won an Oscar, it drew fire for the emotional illogic of Thelma's one-night stand coming right on the heels of her near-rape.

men and women look at — and treat — one another.

Pitt has chosen his directors almost as well as his roles. Besides "Thelma and Louise," Ridley Scott was behind the camera for the sci-fi classics "Alien" and "Blade Runner."

Oscar nominations as Best Actress – though, in retrospect, Sarandon's role, with its hard-earned wisdom and intimations of past suffering, was probably harder to play than Davis' "The Homecoming Queen's Got a Gun" perkiness. To the casual observer, Thelma seems to be the character who changes. Indeed, the arc of her character's transformation is obvious, but Louise changes, too, albeit in a much subtler way. She has spent many years of her life struggling to put her own sexual assault behind her, and now finds that the event has returned to haunt her with a vengeance; through the course of the narrative, she alternates between withdrawal and scrappy confrontation, eventually coming to terms with it and using it as fuel for her righteousness.

Michael Madsen has a few very nice scenes as Louise's beau, who supports her even though he doesn't understand her. Ditto Keitel's cop, who's empathetic and sweet-natured but lets a note of condescension creep into his voice whenever he pronounces the phrase, "those girls."

And of course, the film made a star of Pitt. In the small but pivotal role of J.D., a nomadic armed robber with a bluejeaned ass that could launch a thousand ships, he's a walking cliché, and he appears in a sequence that's both stereotypical and nonsensical. (He gives the repressed Thelma her first orgasm one short day after her attempted rape.) But the lackadaisical glint in Pitt's eye suggests the character is smarter than he pretends to be. He's a smooth operator assuming the guise of a brawny dolt; he uses his looks and charm to get where he wants to be – into Thelma's bed and, later, her purse. ●

b. South Shields, England, 1939.
"Thelma and Louise" (1992). It's helpful to remember that Ridley Scott spent more than a decade making commercials before making his mark as a director. He seems to have sensed the potential latent in Brad Pitt when he walked on the set of "Thelma and Louise," for his scant few scenes play like an extended commercial intended to sell the next great star of the cinema. The posing, the lighting, the dialogue all shout "BUY ME, BUY ME."

RiDLeY SCott

SUSAN
SARANDON

b. Edison, New Jersey, 1946.
"Thelma and Louise" (1992).
One normally expects a former
Ford model to step into lead
parts right out of the box —
and work herself right out of a
job within a few years.
Sarandon reversed the process.
She spent nearly two decades
playing the characters dis-
dained by other leading ladies,
only to find herself hitting her
stride in early middle age.
Beginning in 1988, she was
nominated for Academy
Awards or Golden Globes for
her roles in "Bull Durham,"
"White Palace," "Thelma and
Louise," "Lorenzo's Oil," and
"The Client" before finally winning for "Dead Man Walking."

Too Young to Die

This made-for-TV movie foreshadows the arc of Brad Pitt's career, alternating beautiful parts with dark.

This 1990 made-for-TV movie is sharply written, tautly directed and better acted than most efforts of its type; it also foreshadows the arc of Brad Pitt's subsequent career, which would alternate matinee-idol roles with darker, more perverse character parts. Conceived as a star vehicle for then 16-year-old Juliette Lewis, the script, which was inspired by a true story, concerns a 14-year-old runaway named Amanda Sue Bradley whose unlikely murder of an Army officer would make her the youngest person every put on death row in Oklahoma.

The early tragedies of Mandy's life are dealt with quickly: her childhood in a home with a shallow, ignorant mother and a stepfather who repeatedly raped her; her doomed marriage to a high school sweetheart, who abandoned her after three months to join the military; and her attempts to stay alive by working as an exotic dancer in Tulsa. She hitchhiked there in search of her husband, whom she hoped to locate at a nearby Army base. She becomes romantically involved with a redneck Svengali named Billy Canton (Pitt) who first hooked her up with the exotic dancing job; he will later turn her on to pills and heroin.

Mandy's life takes a temporary turn for the better when she's befriended by a divorced Army officer named Mike Medwicky (Michael O'Keefe), who thrashes Billy in her defense, then invites her to live in the spare bedroom of his suburban house.

Mike keeps Mandy at arms' length because she's a minor, but after a while, that particular taboo is crossed anyway; she becomes his full-time lover and part-time surrogate mom to his two young kids, at last achieving the domestic bliss she always craved but could not have. Then Mike's commanding officers discover that Mandy is living with him (thanks to a strategic phone call placed, of course, by Billy) and he tells the girl that she has to move out immediately and stop seeing him, otherwise he will be court-martialed. Her dreams of a normal family life shattered, Mandy falls into deep despair and reunites with Billy, who convinces her to murder Mike and his girlfriend. When the police arrest Billy, he turns state's witness and gives up Mandy in exchange for immunity. The film is narrated as an extended flashback from prison, as Mandy's attorney (Michael Tucker) prepares her ultimately unsuccessful legal defense.

"Too Young to Die" has gained renewed notice mostly because of its two young stars, who met on the set in 1989, fell in love, and stayed together for four sometimes tempestuous years. But it's also worth seeing for its own merits. Chief among them is its sophisticated take on what drove Mandy to murder: the script suggests she was so beaten by life, abused by men virtually from the cradle onward, that her homicidal impulses stemmed less from a violent impulse than a need for cathartic release. The movie says — and Lewis' controlled, incisive, and powerful performance backs this up — that Mandy never felt alive and in control of her own life until she grabbed a knife and threatened the man who robbed her of her dreams of being a "normal" wife, mother and suburban citizen.

Pitt clearly relishes playing Billy Canton, but the character isn't as forceful and absorbing as he had every right to be. The actor's inexperience may be to blame; then again, perhaps anyone would pale if forced to share the screen with Lewis. Despite her youth, she invests the part of Mandy with a stunning array of habits and inflections, as if she'd lived inside this damaged murderer-to-be for

The Favor

her entire adult life. It's a performance of startling perversity and even more startling completeness, and it's not hard to see how it might intimidate Pitt. No matter: By the time he and Lewis reunited onscreen for "Kalifornia," his facility at playing loathsome loners had definitely caught up with hers.

Dismissed by most critics as a lackluster "women's film" upon its initial release, this domestic comedy from director Donald Petrie holds up surprisingly well. It's about the misadventures of a homemaker named Cathy (Harley Jane Kozak) who has two kids and is married to an amiable drudge of a professor named Peter (Bill Pullman) and a single art gallery owner named Emily (Elizabeth McGovern), who has been Cathy's closest confidant since high school. Each woman envies the other: Cathy is dissatisfied with the routine of domestic life and envies Emily's sexual and career freedom; Emily is tired of living the single life and thinks Cathy has nothing to complain about.

When Emily makes a trip to Denver, Cathy asks her to visit her old high school boyfriend, a jock named Tommy (Ken Wahl), whom Cathy dated but never actually slept with. She asks a favor of Emily: She wants her to sleep with Tommy, then tell her what it was like. Nonplused, Emily ultimately obliges. Rather than vicariously satisfying Cathy's curiosity, her

Cool World

"Cool World" plays like a tawdry remake (minus the imagination) of "Who Framed Roger Rabbit."

descriptions of sexual bliss only make Cathy more obsessed; soon she's making plans to go to Denver and sleep with Tommy herself, and her behavior becomes more erratic by the day. A series of stray comments and misheard conversations convinces Peter that Cathy herself is sleeping with Emily's boyfriend, a twentysomething artist named Elliott (Brad Pitt). Elliott, in turn, begins to suspect that Emily is having an long-term affair with Tommy. All the plot threads are resolved in a hyperactive confrontation at Tommy's Denver home, and everybody goes home enlightened and happy.

The cast is quite fine — particularly Kozak, who makes Cathy's desperation both comic and sad, and McGovern, who's marvelously brittle and no-nonsense as Emily. Pitt's role is small and conceived as a stock character (the sweet but dimwitted hunk who pines for a woman too old for him), but he makes the most of it, delivering his lines with ingratiating sarcasm. Early on, he attends a birthday party with Emily in honor of one of Cathy's children. He patiently watches a clown cavort for the children and makes a stab at mixing purple cows, but he's obviously uncomfortable at how little he has to say to suburban family people. "Nice party," he tells Cathy, vainly attempting to make conversation. "I particularly liked the part where Mr. Lucky couldn't find his hat."

Efficiently directed by Petrie and written with low-key wit by Sara Parriott and JoAnne McGibbon, "The Favor" is a solid romantic comedy about fantasies jeopardizing the good things we already possess.

Underground animator Ralph Bakshi's first feature-length effort since 1982's sword-and-sorcery bomb "Fire and Ice," "Cool World" plays like a tawdry remake of "Who Framed Roger Rabbit." It's about an animator named Jack Deems (Gabriel Byrne) — Bakshi-like creator of a grungy cartoon universe called Cool World — who finds himself warping back and forth between our universe and the one he conceived on paper. None of the misadventures that befall him are interesting or coherent.

The main plotline involves Holly Would, an animated blond bombshell who desperately wants to shed her two-dimensionality and become a 'noid (short for humanoid). Having sex with a human will accomplish the feat, and she targets Jack as the right man for the job. Investigating these strange proceedings is Frank Harris (Brad Pitt), a young man from the World War II era mysteriously transported to Cool World after a motorcycle accident killed his mother.

Basically a collection of sub-par animated setpieces strung together willy-nilly, "Cool World" is a disaster; one never knows exactly how or why Jack warps from reality into cartoonland, and nothing that happens in either location gives us reason to care.

Kim Basinger makes a brief appearance as the human incarnation of Holly Would and embarrasses herself, vamping like a hooker trying to wheedle one more line of coke from her pimp; this film effectively derailed her career as a leading lady. Gabriel Byrne, who is given nothing to work with, tries to make Jack Deems as soulful and human as possible, but because he has nothing to latch onto — and almost no actors to play against, since everyone in Cool World is a cartoon who wouldn't be added until postproduction — he mostly wanders around looking vaguely constipated. Pitt fares no better.

Of all the splendors Bakshi hoped to wow the audience with in "Cool World," none is as astonishing as the fact that some of its participants escaped with careers intact.

DENNIS HOPPER

b. *Dodge City, Kansas, 1936.*
"True Romance" (1993). It is
hard to say which aspect of
Dennis Hopper's career —
actor, director, partier — he
will be remembered for. The
guess here is that the third
option best informs his work.
As a director, "Easy Rider" gave
the '60s drug culture its first
box office hit. As an actor, his
experience with drink and
drugs spawned the alcoholic
father in "Hoosiers" and the
psycho Frank in "Blue Velvet."

CREDITS

TOO YOUNG TO DIE?

Produced by King Features Entertainment (distributor)/Von Zerneck-Sertner Films
(1990) Television
Directed by Robert Markowitz
Written by David Hill (also story), George Rubino
Producers:
Susan Weber-Gold, Julie Anne Weitz
Cast
Michael Tucker: Buddy Thornton
Juliette Lewis: Amanda Sue Bradley
Brad Pitt: Billy Canton
Alan Fudge: Mark Calhoun
Emily Longstreth: Jean
Laurie O'Brien: Wanda Sledge
Yvette Heyden
Tom Everett
Michael O'Keefe: Mike Medwicki
Dean Abston: Harvey
J. Stephen Brady: Brian
Mark Davenport: Mickey
Lew Hopson: Star
Annabelle Weenick: Birdie Jewel
Charles C. Stevenson Jr.: Pastor
Charles David Richards: Billings
Hank Woessner: Boss
Tim De Zarn: Patron
Jeremy Bailey: Police Officer
C.W. Hemingway: Gas Station Attendant
Taylor Fry: Sally
Bradley Michael Pierce: Web
Don Pugsley: Booking Officer
James Schendel: Foreman
Redmond Gleeson: Janitor

THELMA & LOUISE

Produced by MGM/Pathe Entertainment/ United International Pictures (UIP)
(1991) Rated R
Directed by Ridley Scott
Written by Callie Khouri
Producers:
Callie Khouri (co-producer), Dean O'Brien (co-producer), Mimi Polk, Ridley Scott
Cast
Susan Sarandon: Louise Sawyer
Geena Davis: Thelma Dickinson
Harvey Keitel: Hal Slocumb
Michael Madsen: Jimmy
Christopher McDonald: Darryl
Stephen Tobolowsky: Max
Brad Pitt: J.D.
Timothy Carhart: Harlan Puckett
Lucinda Jenney: Lena, the Waitress
Jason Beghe: State Trooper
Sonny Carl Davis: Albert
Ken Swofford: Major
Shelly Desai: East Indian Motel Clerk
Carol Mansell: Waitress
Stephen Polk: Surveillance Man
Rob Roy Fitzgerald: Plainclothes Cop
Jack Lindine: L.D. Tech
Michael Delman: Silver Bullet Dancer
Kristel L. Rose: Girl Smoker
Noel Walcott: Mountain Bike Rider
Marco St. John: Truck Driver
Charlie Sexton: Himself

JOHNNY SUEDE

Produced by Miramax Films (distributor)/ Vega Film Productions
(1992) Rated R
Directed by Tom DiCillo
Written by Tom DiCillo
Cast
Brad Pitt: Johnny Suede
Richard Boes: Man in Tuxedo

Cheryl Costa: Woman in Alley
Michael Luciano: Mr. Clepp
Calvin Levels: Deke
Nick Cave: Freak Storm
Ralph Marrero: Bartender
Wilfredo Giovanni Clark: Slick
Alison Moir: Darlette
Peter McRobbie: Flip Doubt
Ron Vawter: Winston
Dennis Parlato: Dalton
Tina Louise: Mrs. Fontaine
Michael Mulheren: Fred Business
Wayne Maugans: Ned Business
Catherine Keener: Yvonne
Joseph Barry: The Cowboy
John David Barone: Bernard
Tom Jarmusch: Conan
Samuel L. Jackson: B-Bop
Evelyn Solann: Old Woman
Ashley Gardner: Ellen
Ahmed Ben Larby: Cab Driver

COOL WORLD (1992)

Produced by Morgan Creek Productions
(1992) Rated PG-13
Directed by Ralph Bakshi
Written by Michael Grais, Mark Victor
Produced by Frank Mancuso Jr.
Cast
Janni Brenn-Lowen: Mom Harris
Brad Pitt: Frank Harris
William Frankfather: Cop
Greg Collins: Cop
Gabriel Byrne: Jack Deebs
Kim Basinger: Holli Would
Michael David Lally: Sparks (voice)
Michele Abrams: Jennifer Malley
Carrie Hamilton: Comic Bookstore Cashier
Stephen Worth: Comic Store Patron
Murray Podwal: Store Patron
Jenine Jennings: Animation Performance
Model Joey Camen: Interrogator (voice)
Maurice LaMarche: Mash (voice)
Gregory Snegoff: Bash (voice)
Candi Milo: Bob (voice)
Charles Adler: Nails (voice)
Patrick Pinney: Bouncer (voice)
Deirdre O'Connell: Isabelle Malley
Frank Sinatra Jr.: Himself
Lamont Jackson: Lucky's Bouncer
Paul Ben-Victor: Valet

A RIVER RUNS THROUGH IT

(1992) Rated PG
Directed by Robert Redford
Written by Richard Friedenberg, Norman MacLean (story)
Producers:
Jake Eberts (executive), Patrick Markey, Robert Redford
Cast
Craig Sheffer: Norman Maclean
Brad Pitt: Paul Maclean
Tom Skerritt: Rev. Maclean
Brenda Blethyn: Mrs. Maclean
Emily Lloyd: Jessie Burns
Edie McClurg: Mrs. Burns
Stephen Shellen: Neal Burns
Vann Gravage: Young Paul
Nicole Burdette: Mabel
Rob Cox: Conroy
Susan Traylor: Rawhide
Michael Cudlitz: Chub
Buck Simmonds: Humph
Fred Oakland: Mr. Burns
David Creamer: Ken Burns
Madonna Reubens: Aunt Sally
John Reubens: Uncle Jimmy

Arnold Richardson: Old Norman
MacIntyre Dixon: Police Sergeant
Rex Kendall: Reporter
William Hootkins: Murphy
Al Richardson: Mr. Murchison
Jess Schwidde: Mr. Sweeney
Chuck Adamson: Harry the Editor
Jack Kroll: Reporter
Martina Kreidl: Secretary at Newspaper
Noah Snyder: Copy Boy at Newspaper
Margot Kiser: Sal
Anne Merren: Hooker at Lolo
Philip A. Braun: Dealer at Lolo
Tracy Mayfield: Bouncer at Lolo
Chuck Tweed: Drunk in Jail
Prudence Johnson: Pavilion Singer
D. Gorton: Pavilion Announcer
Lincoln Quesenberry: Drunk in Alley
Hawk Forssell: Bouncer at Speakeasy
Jacob Snyder: Piano Player
Jim Dunkin: Speakeasy Bartender
Kathy Scharler: Waitress at Speakeasy
Don Jeffery: Black Jack
Byron Dingman: Speakeasy Patron
Cecily Johnson: Speakeasy Patron
Caleb Shiff: Young John
Joseph Gordon-Levitt: Young Norman
Robert Redford: Narrator (voice)

KALIFORNIA

(1993) Rated R
Produced by: PolyGram/Propaganda Films/Viacom Pictures, Directed by Dominic Sena, Written by Stephen Levy (story), Tim Metcalfe
Producers:
Lynn Bigelow (executive),
Jim Kouf (executive), Mitch Sacharoff (co-producer), Kristine J. Schwarz (co-producer)
Cast
Brad Pitt: Early Grayce
Catherine Larson: Teenage Girl
David Milford: Driver
David Duchovny: Brian Kessler
John Zarchen: Peter
David Rose: Eric
Michelle Forbes: Carrie Laughlin
Tommy Chappelle: Old Man
Juliette Lewis: Adele Corners
Judson Vaughn: Parole Officer
Patricia Sill: Carol
Brett Rice: Police Officer
Marisa Raper: Little Girl
Bill Crabb: Middle Aged Farmer
Mary Ann Hagen: Waitress
Jerry G. White: Gas Station Attendant
Sarah Sullivan: Bar Waitress
Eric Stenson: Young Crocker
Gregory Mars Martin: Walter Livesy
Patricia Hunte: Newscaster
Loanne Bishop: Female Officer
Ron Kuhlman: Male Officer
Sierra Pecheur: Mrs. Musgrave
John Dullaghan: Mr. Musgrave
James Michael McDougal: John Diebold

TRUE ROMANCE

(1993) Rated R
Produced by Morgan Creek, Productions/ August Entertainment, Directed by Tony Scott, Written by Quentin Tarantino, Roger Avary (uncredited)
Producers:
Stan Margulies, James G. Robinson, Bob Weinstein, Harvey Weinstein (executives)
Cast
Christian Slater: Clarence Worley

Patricia Arquette: Alabama Worley
Dennis Hopper: Clifford Worley
Val Kilmer: Mentor (Elvis)
Gary Oldman: Drexl Spivey
Brad Pitt: Floyd
Christopher Walken: Vincenzo Coccotti
Bronson Pinchot: Elliot Blitzer
Samuel L. Jackson: Big Don
Michael Rapaport: Dick Ritchie
Saul Rubinek: Lee Donowitz
Conchata Ferrell: Mary Louise Ravencroft
James Gandolfini: Virgil
Anna Levine: Lucy
Victor Argo: Lenny
Paul Bates: Marty
Chris Penn: Nicky Dimes
Tom Sizemore: Cody Nicholson
Said Faraj: Burger Man
Gregory Sporleder: Burger Customer
Maria Pitillo: Kandi
Frank Adonis: Frankie
Kevin Corrigan: Marvin
Paul Ben-Victor: Luca
Michael Beach: Wurlitzer
Joe D'Angerio: Police Radio Operator
John Bower: Detective
John Cenatiempo: Squad Cop #1
Eric Allen Kramer: Boris
Patrick John Hurley: Monty
Dennis Garber: Lobby Cop #1
Scott Evers: Lobby Cop #2
Hilary Klym: Running Cop
Steve Gonzales: L.A. Officer
Laurence Mason: Floyd "D"

THE FAVOR

(1994) Rated R
Produced by Orion Films,
Directed by Donald Petrie,
Written by Josann McGibbon, Sara Parriot
Cast
Harley Jane Kozak: Kathy
Elizabeth McGovern: Emily
Bill Pullman: Peter Whiting
Brad Pitt: Elliott
Larry Miller: Joe Dubin
Ken Wahl: Tom Andrews
Ginger Orsi: Gina
Leigh Ann Orsi: Hannah
Felicia Robertson: Carol
Kenny Twomey: Mr. Lucky
Florence Schauffler: Museum Docent
Elaine Mee: Chunky Woman
John Horn: Pastor
Wilma Bergheim: Ladies at Church
Mary Marsh: Ladies at Church
Marilyn Blechschmidt: Mrs. Konzulman
Sharon Collar: Clerk at Drugstore
Carl King: Man at Drugstore
Deborah White: Professor Allen
Lisa Robins: Stewardess
Arthur Burghardt: Hotel Clerk
Michael Anthony Taylor: Bootsie
Steve Kahan: Helpful Fisherman
Robert Biheller: Fishermen
Gary Powell: Fishermen
Moultrie Patten: Peter's Cabbie
Joel Beeson: Young Tom Andrews
Paul Beeson: Young Tom Andrews
Susan Zeitlin: Birthday Party Guests
Michelle Robinson: Birthday Party Guests
Dylan Taylor: Birthday Party Guests
Doug Baldwin: Birthday Party Guests
Kim Walker: Jill Topial
Claire Stansfield: Miranda
O-Lan Jones: Mrs. Moyer
Milt Oberman: Mr. Moyer

Heather Morgan: Linda
Mindy Sterling: Debbie Rollins
Jordan Christopher Michael: Alex
Holland Taylor: Maggie Sand

LEGENDS OF THE FALL
(1994) Rated R
Produced by Pangaea/TriStar/Bedford Falls,
Directed by Edward Zwick, Written by Jim
Harrison (novel), Susan Shilliday, William
D. Wittliff
Producers:
Patrick Crowley, William D. Wittliff,
Edward Zwick
Cast
Brad Pitt: Tristan Ludlow (GGN)
Anthony Hopkins: Col. Ludlow
Aidan Quinn: Alfred
Julia Ormond: Susannah
Henry Thomas: Samuel
Karina Lombard: Isabel Two
Tantoo Cardinal: Pet
Gordon Tootoosis: One Stab
Paul Desmond: Decker
Christina Pickles: Isabel
Robert Wisden: John T. O'Banion
John Novak: James O'Banion
Kenneth Welsh: Sheriff Tynert
Bill Dow: Longley
Sam Sarkar: Rodriguez
Nigel Bennett: Asgaard
Deegan Macintosh: Boy Tristan
Eric Johnson: Teen Tristan
Randall Slavin: Teen Alfred
Doug Hughes: Teen Samuel
Sekwan Auger: Young Isabel Two
David Kaye: Samuel Decker
Christine Harder: Isabel Three
Charles Andre (II): Federal Officer
Weston McMillan: Noel
Aaron Goettel: Corporal's Friend
Brian Stollery: Captain
Bill Croft: Bartender
Ray Godshall: Businessman
Marc Levy: Butler
Ken Zirzinger: O'Banion Thug
Winnie Hung: Chinese Woman
Simon Sherwood: Officer
Rob Hrdlicka: Canadian Soldier
Channing Knull: Canadian Soldier
Matt Huson: German Soilder
John D. Cameron: Proprietor

INTERVIEW WITH THE VAMPIRE
(1994) Rated R
Produced by Geffen Pictures, Directed by
Neil Jordan, Written by Anne Rice
Producers:
David Geffen, Stephen Woolley
Redmond Morris (co-producer)
Cast
Brad Pitt: Louis
Christian Slater: Malloy (The Interviewer)
Tom Cruise: Lestat
Stephen Rea: Santiago
Antonio Banderas: Armand
Kirsten Dunst: Claudia
Virginia McCollam: Whore on Waterfront
John McConnell: Gambler
Mike Seelig: Pimp
Bellina Logan: Tavern Girl
Thandie Newton: Yvette
Lyla Hay Owen: Widow St. Clair
Lee Emery: Widow's Lover
Indra Ove: New Orleans Whore
Helen McCrory: 2nd New Orleans Whore
Monte Montague: Plague Victim Bearer

Nathalie Bloch: Maid
Jeanette Kontomitras: Woman in Square
Roger Lloyd Pack: Piano Teacher
George Kelly: Dollmaker
Nicole Dubois: Creole Woman
Micha Bergese: Paris Vampire
Rory Edwards: Paris Vampire
Marcel Iures: Paris Vampire
Susan Lynch: Paris Vampire
Louise Salter: Paris Vampire
Matthew Sim: Paris Vampire
Francois Testory: Paris Vampire
Andrew Tiernan: Paris Vampire
Simon Tyrrell: Paris Vampire
George Yiasoumi: Paris Vampire
Sara Stockbridge: Estelle
Laure Marsac: Mortal Woman on Stage
Katia Caballero: Woman in Audience
Louis Lewis-Smith: Mortal Boy
Domiziana Giordano: Madeleine

TWELVE MONKEYS
(1995) Rated R
Produced by Atlas, Entertainment/
Universal Pictures,Directed by Terry
Gilliam, Written by David Webb Peoples,
Janet Peoples, Chris Marker
Producers:
Robert Cavallo, Robert Kosberg,
Gary Levinsohn
Cast
Bruce Willis: James Cole
Madeleine Stowe: Dr. Kathryn Railly
Brad Pitt: Jeffrey Goines (S:AAN) (S:GG)
Christopher Plummer: Dr. Goines
Joseph Melito: Young Cole
Jon Seda: Jose
Michael Chance: Scarface
Vernon Campbell: Tiny
H. Michael Walls: Botanist
Bob Adrian: Geologist
Simon Jones (I): Zoololgist
Carol Florence: Astrophysicist
Bill Raymond: Microbiologist
Ernest Abuba: Engineer
Irma St. Paule: Poet
Joey Perillo: Detective Franki
Bruce Kirkpatrick: Policeman#1
Wilfred Williams: Policeman#2
Rozwill Young: Billings
Nell Johnson: Ward Nurse
Fred Strother: L.J. Washington
Rick Warner: Dr. Casey
Frank Gorshin: Dr. Fletcher
Anthony 'Chip' Brienza: Dr. Goodin
Joilet Harris: Harassed Mother
Drucie McDaniel: Waltzing Woman Patient
John Blaisse: Old Man Patient
Louis Lippa: Patient at Gate
Stan Kang: X-Ray Doctor
Pat Dias: WWI Captain
Aaron Michael Lacey: WWI Sergeant
David Morse: Dr. Peters
Charles Techman: Professor
Jann Ellis: Marilou
Johnnie Hobbs Jr.: Officer No. 1
Janet Zappala: Anchorwoman
Thomas Roy: Evangelist
Harry O'Toole: Louie
Korchenko: Thug
Chuck Jeffreys: Thug
Lisa Gay Hamilton: Teddy
Felix A. Pire: Fale
Mathew Ross: Bee
Barry Price: Agent
John Panzarella: Agent
Larry Daly: Agent
Arthur Fennell: Anchorman

Karl Warren: Pompous Man
Christopher Meloni: Lt. Halperin
Paul Meshejian: Detective Dalva
Robert O'Neill: Wayne
Kevin Thigpen: Kweskin
Lee Golden: Hotel Clerk
Joseph McKenna: Wallace
Jeff Tanner: Plain Clothes Cop
Faith Potts: Store Clerk
Michael Ryan Segal: Weller
Annie Golden: Woman Cabbie
Lisa Talerico: Ticket Agent
Stephen Bridgewater: Airport Detective
Franklin Huffman: Plump Businessman
Joann S. Dawson: Gift Store Clerk
Jack Dougherty: Airport Security
Lenny Daniels: Airport Security
Herbert C. Hauls Jr.: Airport Security
Charley Scalies: Impatient Traveler
Carolyn Walker: Terrified Traveler

SE7EN
(1995) Rated R
Produced by New Line Cinema, Directed
by David Fincher, Written by Andrew
Kevin Walker
Producers:
Dan Kolsrud (executive), Anne Kopelson
(executive), Gianni Nunnari (executive)
Cast
Brad Pitt: David Mills
Morgan Freeman: William Somerset
Gwyneth Paltrow: Tracy Mills
Richard Roundtree: Talbot
R. Lee Ermey: Police Captain
John C. McGinley: California
Julie Araskog: Mrs Gould
Mark Boone Junior: Greasy FBI Man
John Cassini: Officer Davis
Reg E. Cathey: Coroner
Peter Crombie: Dr O'Neill
James Hawthorne: George,
Library Night Guard
Michael Massee: Man in Massage
Parlour Booth
Leland Orser: Crazed Man in
Massage Parlour
Richard Portnow: Dr Beardsley
Richard Schiff: Mark Swarr
Pamala Tyson: Thin Vagrant
Kevin Spacey: John Doe
Endre Hules: Cab Driver
Andy Walker: Dead Man
Daniel Zacapa: Detective Taylor
Bob Mack: Gluttony Victim
George Christy: Workman
Roscoe Davidson: Library Guard
Bob Collins: Library Guard
Jimmy Dale Hartsell: Library Janitor
Charline Su: TV News Reporter
Dominique Jennings: TV News Reporter
Allan Kolman: Forensic Man
Beverly Burke: TV Anchor Woman
Gene Borkan: Eli Gould (Sin of Greed)
Mdario Di Donato: Fingerprint
Forensic Man
Alfonso Freeman: Fingerprint Technician
Harrison White: Cop on SWAT Team
Robert Stephenson: Cop on SWAT Team
Michael Reid MacKay: Victor (Sin of Sloth)
Tudor Sherrard: Coupon Man
Lennie Leftin: Policeman
Sarah Hale Reinhardt: Police Sketch Artist
Emily Wagner: Detective Sara
Martin Serene: Wild Bill
David Correia: Cop at Massage Parlour
Ron Blair: Cop at Massage Parlour
Cat Mueller: Hooker (Sin of Lust)

Lexie Bigham: Sweating Cop
at Massage Parlour
Evan Miranda: Paramedic
Paul S. Eckstein: Paramedic
Heidi Schanz: Beautiful Woman
(Sin of Pride)
Brian Evers: Duty Sergeant
Shannon Wilcox: Cop Behind Desk
Jim Deeth: Helicopter Pilot
John Stantini: Helicopter Pilot
Charles A. Tamburro: SWAT Helicopter Pilot
Richmond Arquette: Delivery Man
Duffy Gaver: Marksman in Helicopter
Andrew Kevin Walker: Opening Scene
Corpse (uncredited)

SLEEPERS
(1996) Rated R
Directed by Barry Levinson, Written by
Barry Levinson,Lorenzo Carcaterra (novel)
Producers:
Barry Levinson, Steve Golin
Cast
Zach Ansley: Burly Man
Peter Appel: Boyfriend
Kevin Bacon: Nokes
William Butler (I): Juanito
Billy Crudup: Tommy
Robert De Niro: Father Bobby
Jeffrey Donovan: Addison
Minnie Driver: Carol Martinez
Ron Eldard: John
Vittorio Gassman: King Benny
Peter Gerety: Juvenile Lawyer
Saverio Guerra: 2nd Man
Ben Hammer: Judge Weisman
Dustin Hoffman: Danny O'Connor
Terry Kinney: Ferguson
Bruno Kirby: Shakes' Father
Daniel Mastrogiorgio: Nick Davenport
Mary B. McCann: Sister Carolyn
Frank Medrano: Fat Mancho
Michael Moran: Juvenile Judge
Jason Patric: Shakes
Joseph Perrino: Young Shakes
James Pickens Jr.: Marlboro
Wendell Pierce: Little Caesar
Brad Pitt: Michael Sullivan
Monica Polito: Young Carol
Sean Reilly: Young King Benny
Brad Renfro: Young Michael Sullivan
Peter Rini: Frank
Larry Romano: 1st Man
Gayle Scott: Confession Woman
Tom Signorelli: Confession Man
John Slattery: Fred Carlson
Henry Stram: Prison Doctor
Jonathan Tucker: Young Tommy
Aida Turturro: Mrs Salinas
Joe Urla: Carson
Geoffrey Wigdor: Young John

DEVIL'S OWN
(1997) Rated R
Directed by Alan J. Pakula, Written by
Kevin Jarre, Robert Kamen, Alan J. Pakula,
Terry George
Producer:
Larry Gordon
Cast
Harrison Ford: Tom O'Meara
Brad Pitt: Frankie the Angel
Ruben Blades
Treat Williams
Margaret Colin
George Hearn
Kelly Singer
Julia Stiles

CONTRIBUTORS

THE WRITER

Matt Zoller Seitz writes a Sunday column about popular culture for the *Newark Star-Ledger* and is a film critic for the weekly *New York Press*. His work has appeared in *The New York Times*, *Newsday*, *Dallas Observer*, *Houston Press*, *Seattle Weekly*, and the online entertainment magazine *Mr. Showbiz*. He and his wife live in New York City with two badly behaved cats.

THE PHOTOGRAPHERS